Embrace Makerspace

Embrace Makerspace

A Pocket Guide for Elementary School Administrators

Randee Bonagura

ROWMAN & LITTLEFIELD
Lanham • Boulder • New York • London

Published by Rowman & Littlefield
A wholly owned subsidiary of The Rowman & Littlefield Publishing Group, Inc.
4501 Forbes Boulevard, Suite 200, Lanham, Maryland 20706
www.rowman.com

Unit A, Whitacre Mews, 26-34 Stannary Street, London SE11 4AB

Copyright © 2017 by Randee Bonagura

All rights reserved. No part of this book may be reproduced in any form or by any electronic or mechanical means, including information storage and retrieval systems, without written permission from the publisher, except by a reviewer who may quote passages in a review.

British Library Cataloguing in Publication Information Available

Library of Congress Cataloging-in-Publication Data Available

Names: Bonagura, Randee, 1974– author.
Title: Embrace makerspace : a pocket guide for elementary school administrators / Randee Bonagura.
Description: Lanham : Rowman & Littlefield, , a wholly owned subsidiary of The Rowman & Littlefield Publishing Group, Inc., [2017].
Identifiers: LCCN 2016042601| ISBN 9781475828900 (cloth : alk. paper) | ISBN 9781475828917 (pbk. : alk. paper) | ISBN 9781475828924 (electronic)
Subjects: LCSH: Maker movement in education. | Makerspaces. | Education, Elementary—United States.
Classification: LCC LB1029.M35 B66 2017 | DDC 371.39—dc23 LC record available at https://lccn.loc.gov/2016042601

∞ ™ The paper used in this publication meets the minimum requirements of American National Standard for Information Sciences Permanence of Paper for Printed Library Materials, ANSI/NISO Z39.48-1992.

Printed in the United States of America

Contents

Acknowledgments — vii
Introduction — ix

1. Collaboration — 1
2. Philosophy in Action — 11
3. Creating and Cultivating Space — 21
4. Developing a Supply Stream — 35
5. Scheduling, Staffing, and Professional Development — 43
6. Budget and Branding — 51
7. Assessment — 63
8. The Journey Ahead — 75

Appendix — 79
References — 89
About the Author — 91

Acknowledgments

This book began as a personal journal chronicling my adventure through the process of bringing makerspace to the school where I am grateful to serve as principal. Along this journey from an empty nook and a trunk full of craft items to a classroom filled with materials where students excitedly create prototypes and inventions, I have learned so much about collaboration and reflection from my school community.

I want to thank my colleagues who courageously embraced makerspace and contributed ideas, enthusiasm, and supplies to this new endeavor, and who continue to research and design new projects for our students. I want to especially thank Jessica Zimmer for her creativity, intelligence, and perseverance. I am fortunate to work with such talented and dedicated educators and to have the support of our administration and board of education.

Thank you to our students, who have come into makerspace, designed transportation of the future, helped the Gingerbread Man cross the river in creative ways, engineered penguin habitats, and suggested new projects. It is the children and their families that make our space exciting and meaningful.

Thank you to my husband who lovingly asks if I want to save more paper towel rolls to use in makerspace, to my daughters who inspire me as they turn recyclables into art, and to my parents for always believing in me. I am grateful for the love and unconditional support of my family, without which this project would not have been possible.

I want to thank my editors for their feedback and thoughtful assistance throughout the process of creating this book and for taking a leap of faith and making my relationship with Rowman & Littlefield possible.

Introduction

Makerspace is a place where students can engage in creative experiences to solve problems, tinker, design, learn new skills, and be entrepreneurial. Individually or in groups, students can work on projects that involve STEAM (science, technology, engineering, art, and math) concepts that align with state and national curriculum standards. It is a place that encourages risk taking, revision, and reflection and is stocked with materials that provide equal access to all learners.

Makerspace is a shared learning environment where students follow the design process as they learn and teach each other with the guidance and encouragement of teachers, adult volunteers, or other staff. Makerspace can be in any location in your school, ranging from a box or rolling cart filled with basic craft supplies to an entire room stocked with the newest technology. Students can create prototypes and discoveries that are arguably just as meaningful made with no-tech rubber bands and clothespins or with high-tech 3D printers and robots. Makerspace can be used intermittently or frequently and can involve a variety of staffing and scheduling options. This guide will offer ideas for you to consider relating to supplies, professional development, teaching and learning philosophies, budget, assessment, and other resources as you create and enhance makerspace.

Your makerspace reflects the culture of your school and district, your leadership style, the needs of your students, and the resources available. Each school is different; each makerspace is unique. As an administrator, you will play a large role in the five *W*s and the *H* of makerspace:

- **Who** from the school and larger community will be involved in this initiative?
- **What** materials and supplies will be stocked in makerspace?
- **Why** is makerspace needed in your school?
- **When** will it be used throughout the year?
- **Where** will makerspace be located within your building?

- **How** will you promote and expand makerspace so it is a continuing success?

You already have many decisions to make each day, week, and year. You are responsible for curriculum implementation, selecting and evaluating staff, budgeting and purchasing, professional development, student discipline and safety, maintenance concerns, special events, community relations, and just about anything else that happens in and around your school. The decision to create makerspace creatively integrates all of these components and will reap tangible and intangible rewards for students, staff, and the community, as well as provide opportunities for you to grow as a professional educator.

Bringing makerspace to your school is a way to lead by example and will truly make you the principal maker. You will be solving problems to develop a schedule for students and teachers to interact in this new space, and designing and redesigning the makerspace location as new materials are donated and purchased. You may find yourself tinkering with new ideas as you research projects on Pinterest and Instructables late into the evening and catching up on the latest blogs and Twitter feeds about everything related to maker culture.

You may learn new skills such as how to operate button makers and book binders, code robots big and small, as well as stock every size and shape battery you can find to facilitate wearable circuit projects. Your skills as a marketer, event planner, product merchandiser, and social media guru will grow exponentially as you promote the hard work of your staff and students, which will transform into your unique community of makers.

This guide is intended to help you plan and implement a makerspace that is the best fit for your school. There is no right or wrong way to create makerspace. There is no better or worse way to schedule makerspace to be utilized. Materials and supplies are neither good nor bad. Follow the lead of your students and staff, clarify your guiding philosophy of teaching and learning, evaluate your resources, and prepare to make a difference in the lives of those who share your school community.

ONE
Collaboration

A makerspace initiative provides a unique opportunity for school administrators to unite a variety of constituents to work toward a common student-centered goal. It is important to coordinate this undertaking with your board of education, central administrators, clerical staff, custodians, department supervisors, and chairpersons, teachers, and parent organization. While this may seem like a diverse group, casting a wide net will make available resources and support that you may not have envisioned nor had access to independently. Each group and every person within these groups likely has a personal skill set, hobbies, and outside interests that will add value to your initiative when they are welcomed to be part of makerspace.

Inviting participation broadens and improves the overall opportunity you provide to your students and strengthens creative bonds across the community. Reach out to these people and groups, explain your vision for makerspace, and see how they can support your school and, in return, how your makerspace initiative can support their work.

BOARD OF EDUCATION

A principal's role is to support and implement the policies and practices established by the board of education. Gaining their support is of the utmost importance to be able to continue plans for implementation. There are several steps principals can take to share their vision:

- Review your district's current annual goals to see how a makerspace initiative can be significantly aligned. The recent emphasis on twenty-first-century skills, STEAM (science, technology, engineering, art, and math), and college and career readiness support the central tenets of makerspace. National curriculum standards provide many connections between district goals and a makerspace undertaking.
- You may want to put together a written proposal or visual presentation to share with your board of education that provides an overview of the initiative. There are many articles and video clips available on the Internet about makerspaces that can be readily included. The International Society for Technology Education (http://www.iste.org/), the New York Hall of Science (http://nysci.org/), and Make (http://makezine.com/) are all prominent resources that you will find helpful and that will lead you to dig deeper into the world of making.
- Formally or informally invite members of the board of education to spend time with you and your elementary school students in makerspace as you begin this ever-evolving initiative. Act as a tour guide and explain the resources currently available and the resources you are hoping to add in the future. Encourage board members to share their skills with students at a later date, as they may have expertise in engineering, handicrafts, or many other areas that they can teach to young students. You may want to create a map or diagram of your proposed space, or a brochure with details to enhance the tour and help members of the board remember key features after the visit ends.

CENTRAL ADMINISTRATORS

The superintendent of schools and assistant superintendent(s), along with business administrators, will be important people who can help makerspace become a reality. Reach out to them early and often about protocols regarding purchasing and professional development opportunities.

- The superintendent and assistant superintendent can help arrange for site visits for you and staff members to go to schools that have active makerspaces, by reaching out to their network of colleagues. Research nearby locations that you'd like to visit and suggest these as options. In addition to schools, libraries and museums have makerspaces that would inspire ideas that can easily transfer to an elementary school setting. Some nearby middle and high schools, and even colleges, may have makerspaces that you can visit, keeping an eye on how you would adapt what you see to an elementary school setting.

- Central administrators can facilitate your attendance at upcoming conferences and webinars so you can gather additional information to help your initiative succeed. Seek out opportunities through any professional organizations or groups you belong to, join any that now seem pertinent but previously hadn't been on your radar, search popular professional development companies that send mailings with relevant upcoming workshops, and reach out to local institutions such as museums and corporations that have helped launch makerspaces. Attend Edcamps, maker expos, and related local events at other public venues to gather practical ideas, either in person or by visiting their websites.
- Work closely with your central administrators to help promote professional learning communities (PLCs) among other administrators throughout your district who may also be exploring makerspaces in their schools. Suggest current texts, articles, and videos to be shared and collaborate among colleagues. Search TED Talks, Edutopia, Make, Teacher Librarian, Renovated Learning, and similar Internet sites for current trends and information.
- The business office can provide information about approved vendors for when you want to purchase new or uncommon items, possibly from sole-source companies. They can help with bids, quotes, and state contract discounts so your budget can stretch as far as possible, helping increase the resources you can make available to students. Be sure to contact the seller regarding any warranties on electronic or robotic supplies and have that information included in your quote.

A successful makerspace needs coordination among many offices. By working together with central administrators, a building principal can launch this initiative. At the building level, there are many staff members that will be of great assistance as well, including clerical staff, custodians, department supervisors who work with your school, and of course your teaching staff.

CLERICAL STAFF

Main office secretaries, library clerks, greeters, or any other staff member who interacts with students and parents can play a positive role in promoting makerspace. Very often these staff members have extensive knowledge about procedures and protocols.

- Clerical staff members can help direct students and parents to where to put donations and will alert you to any questions or concerns. They may be able to help organize and inventory items, send out letters and lists for donation requests, and track spending related to equipment and supplies.
- Include the clerical staff in conversations about needed items as they may likely have knowledge about what may be in storage, on order, or what can be repurposed and recycled for use in makerspace.

The clerical staff's deep understanding of the school's history and community resources is an asset not to be overlooked. These staff members may also be able to help with the budgeting and purchasing logistics, as well as preparing newsletters and mailings related to makerspace. They will likely have practical suggestions and be willing to help you succeed, especially if they have a special interest in this undertaking.

CUSTODIANS

The custodians, buildings and grounds crew, and facilities director are truly the movers and shakers that help makerspace take shape. With permission and planning, the custodial staff can paint the room, maneuver furniture, move heavy boxes of supplies and equipment, install anything that needs mounting, and maintain the overall cleanliness of the space.

- The custodial staff may have expertise in areas that will help expand makerspace offerings. Be sure to include them when you ask members of the school community if they have skills or hobbies they would like to share with students. You may

likely find that the custodians are excellent craftsmen, artists, and musicians and have other valuable talents.
- Include the custodial staff when brainstorming a list of supplies to purchase or that you will request to be donated. They may have innovative ideas for additional resources, as well as knowledge of materials that are currently in the school that may be available to use or repurpose.
- Check with the head custodian and director of facilities regarding any safety regulations that need to be in place. Ensure that everything in makerspace is up to code and permitted in a school setting. This is especially important if you will be working with any chemicals or flammable materials, machinery, or electric tools.

Communicate with your custodians often to get their perspective on ways to improve the makerspace logistics. They may have suggestions for organizing materials that help keep the room neater, ways to better utilize space, and requests to help keep the room cleaner, leading to a more streamlined learning environment.

DEPARTMENTAL SUPERVISORS AND CHAIRPERSONS

Makerspace is often part of the STEAM curriculum, integrating various content areas. As the building leader, it is important for you to reach out and include the department supervisors and chairpersons of the disciplines involved. Each of these curriculum specialists will be able to lend something unique to enhance makerspace.

- Each curriculum department leader will likely belong to professional organizations related to their specific field of study. They may have publications and resources that can be shared with you and modified to fit an elementary school makerspace.
- Department heads often have grants, contests, and workshops that come their way and can now be on the lookout for opportunities that support makerspace. Encourage them to share with you anything they think may be valuable. You may want to co-author a grant application, publicize a contest together, or attend workshops with teachers from their department to broaden your perspective.
- Understanding how a makerspace in an elementary school will fit the needs of students when they enter the upper

grades is crucial. Spending time with secondary school staff members can illuminate some of these connections, and a department supervisor can help facilitate a visit for you to a math, science, art, music, family and consumer science, and technology class in middle or high school.

- Invite department leaders to spend time with students and teachers in your school. Ask for feedback about materials they would suggest adding to makerspace and about any new programs you can investigate together. Discover ways that makerspace can align skills and strategies your students will need in the upper grades that can be included in upcoming projects and activities.
- Find out if department heads would be willing to put out an "all call" for materials and supplies that are no longer used by their department and that can used for makerspace. Often, when new standards are adopted or when enrollment changes, materials shift regarding which grade levels they are intended for or sometimes get discarded. Work together to gather anything usable and repurpose it in makerspace as raw materials or as an investigation station, as long as the items are safe and age appropriate.

Departmental supervisors and chairpersons are the local content experts. Use their experience and specific vantage points to add a diverse array of materials and challenging projects for your students. Science, technology, engineering, art, and math may be supervised by various people, but your vision for makerspace can be the reason to bring them all together.

TEACHERS

Classroom teachers are integral to makerspace becoming an embedded part of the school's culture. As the building principal, identifying teachers' varying readiness levels for change in general and gauging their anticipated interest in makerspace are important early steps. Any or all of the ideas here can help engage teachers.

- Develop a survey, either online or on paper, asking teachers what they know about makerspace, how they feel about makerspace in their school, how often they would consider using it with their class, and other questions that will help guide

planning. Analyze the results, and plan your professional development accordingly.
- Share your passion for creativity and tinkering with staff. Develop hands-on problem-solving activities to do with teachers at faculty meetings, as well as open-ended activities they can try with students. Ask for feedback about what went well and suggestions for improvement. YouTube and TED talks are excellent resources for ideas to engage your faculty. The Marshmallow Challenge and Caine's Arcade are two inspiring projects to know about, and all you really need is some dry spaghetti or cardboard to make it happen.
- Provide opportunities for all teachers to be part of the makerspace research and planning stages. You may find that art, music, physical education, library, and computer teachers are very interested.
- Consider creating a makerspace committee with planning sessions dedicated to implementing and evaluating the initiative. Interested teachers would be likely to join, and their input is so valuable to ensuring that the room, and the program, is practical and grounded.
- Organize tours of the space to be used, and invite staff members to help with the design and logistics of what goes where.
- Begin a professional learning community focused on makerspace articles, blogs, texts, and Twitter feeds that can be shared with those interested.
- Invite interested teachers to go on site visits to other schools or locations that have makerspaces.
- Give teachers information about makerspace in advance, before sending notes home with students, so they can help promote the changing needs of makerspace. If you are sending home a list of requested supplies, information about nearby maker events, or a parent letter about makerspace in general, let teachers have an opportunity to digest the details and share it with students so it is more than just one of many notices that go in a folder that gets sent home. Teachers can help build excitement among students for makerspace, and hopefully students will share that excitement with their families.

Teachers are on the frontline of all new initiatives. It is imperative to meet their needs in order for a new idea to be successful, since so many new curriculum changes come their way. If teachers need time, information, coaching, flexibility, support, or other resources, you are there to provide it. Makerspace is a change, and even positive changes can take time to blossom.

PARENT ORGANIZATIONS

Working together with parent organizations such as a PTA or PTO, moms or dads club, grade-level or room representatives, or other established system for parent participation in the school is an ideal way to start to involve parents in the makerspace initiative. This is a case where the more "hands-on" and the more "minds-on" you have, the better the result will be.

- Make a presentation at a parent-organization meeting to share information about makerspace. It can be a visual presentation that includes videos and photos or a handout that has information and ideas. If you made a presentation for your board of education or central administrators, you can use that as a springboard for a parent presentation.
- Send a notice home, use e-mail and/or social media to invite parents to be part of a makerspace committee. You can discuss project ideas, materials, and community resources. Parents may be able to gather supplies to donate, suggest guest workshop presenters, or share sources in town that can provide tools for making.
- Create a brief survey for parents asking if they want to volunteer their time and talents in makerspace. Many parents want to share their professional skills as well as their hobbies in their children's school and can often spare an hour or so sometime during the school year, if scheduled in advance.
- Offer the option for parents or family members to help from home. They can prepare materials for upcoming makerspace projects and send the items in to school ready to be used.
- Suggest to parents other opportunities to be involved in makerspace. Some may be able to help organize supplies, write grants, assist students who are working on a project, prepare materials, or research new ideas to add to a project library. Some may want to take photos or videos of students in action, add to a school website or social media outlet, or promote student learning in other ways. (Be sure to account for any students with privacy issues and those who cannot be photographed or recorded as per district policy.)

Parents are an influential source of assistance and support. Including them through existing parent-organization structures and reaching out to them through presentations, surveys, invitations, and informational notices will likely capture the attention of many who are interested in being part of the makerspace initiative. Providing various ways to help that include donating supplies, sharing expertise, or spending time helping at the school creates an inclusive culture that makes it possible for many parents to be involved in a way that meets their family's needs.

Elementary school principals communicate with these various groups fluidly. Adding makerspace as a topic to communicate about adds another dimension to their interactions. Principals need to share their successes and the areas where they need some help. Makerspace creates an interdisciplinary, creative, home-school connection and broadens everyone's understanding of what types of learning are valued in an educational environment. Encouraging more people and groups to participate expands the range of opportunities that can be offered to students.

TWO
Philosophy in Action

As you gain approval from the board of education, attend site visits and conferences, and read articles, it is important to focus on your philosophy guiding the implementation of makerspace. As the building leader, this initiative outwardly reflects your intrinsic ideas and beliefs about teaching and learning. Ask yourself these questions, as they will impact how you establish space; send out a list of supply donations needed; offer professional development; consider scheduling and staffing options, budget, and branding; and assess your makerspace:

- How does makerspace fit within your school *climate and culture*?
- How does makerspace align with your core *beliefs about learning*?
- How will makerspace meet the needs of *diverse learners*?

Your personal responses may include a variety of pedagogies and values. It is important to have a clear rationale for implementing makerspace, and this rationale will likely become your mantra as you forge ahead. Think deeply about culture and climate, beliefs about learning, and diverse learners. Consider these guiding elements, and then plan to expand your makerspace accordingly.

Chapter 2

CULTURE AND CLIMATE

It is important to recognize the embedded culture of your school, which includes the degree of competition and comparison that exists in your school, the unwritten rules that exist, as well as how much students and staff contribute to decision making (Loukas 2007). Culture goes hand in hand with climate, which includes the mood, morale, and attitudes of the school, and describes how people feel day to day (Gruenert 2008). Every school has a unique way of doing things; student and staff attitudes about new initiatives and feelings about change vary.

Makerspace can be successful in any culture with any climate, and your makerspace needs to be the right fit for your school. By creating an inviting and positive climate, your makerspace initiative can become part of the culture of your school. Makerspace offers opportunities for projects that include cooperation among teachers and students, as well as across grade levels and schools.

As the building leader, you can help transform a competitive staff into a collaborative team. For example, older students can be paired with students in a younger class to make a new toy, invent a new kind of transportation, or create a project that extends a common unit of study in some way. Create a makerspace binder filled with clear page protectors so staff can add project ideas to share with others. Encourage staff to attend STEAM conferences together and then pass on what they learned to colleagues. Invite older students to be helpers in makerspace during lunch and/or recess to assist younger students, or teachers, or to sort and organize supplies. Create a bulletin board for all to see that showcases makerspace projects and processes, so that it looks inviting and within everyone's reach.

To help build or grow a collaborative climate, the school can focus its makerspace projects on a local organization in need of help, such as a food pantry or pet shelter. Each grade level can work on a project that involves STEAM and contribute to that organization. Then, come together to share what each grade level made, as it is ready to be donated. Examples include using a button maker or card-making supplies to add notes of encouragement to people in our armed forces or thank-you notes to volunteers at an organization, creating safe items for pets at an animal shelter such as toys or blankets, or making seasonal crafts to be included in packages at a local food pantry or as welcome gifts for those in need of housing. Using makerspace as a way to give back to the community touches on so many invisible curriculum areas such as character education, and each project inherently includes reading, following directions, listening, and math, science, and engineering, even if in a rudimentary way.

Students and staff can be part of the decision making regarding makerspace supplies, projects, organization, and scheduling as much or as little as is appropriate for your school's culture and climate. You can include a suggestion box or board where teachers and students can add ideas. You can have a committee that includes however many members is the right amount for your school, and you can meet as often as is comfortable. Some schools will have many members and many meetings, and others will have few-to-no members and fewer meetings. Shared decision making in whatever form fits will help provide a forum for anyone who wants to make a positive impact on growing the makerspace opportunity for students and your school community.

The culture of your school will indicate whether staff will stay after or come before school to be part of makerspace meetings or workshops, if teachers will volunteer some of their lunch or preparation time on their own to create new projects, or if they will participate during contractual time only. Be sure to consider collective bargaining agreements before planning meetings so that you can maximize staff participation and honor the existing culture of the school. When your makerspace takes off as an exciting program that more teachers want to be part of, the culture in your school may shift. This may take time, as change doesn't happen overnight, or necessarily over one academic year. As the culture shifts, the climate will likely become one that encourages risk taking and student-centered, enjoyable learning experiences.

You may want to delegate a specific person to research and order supplies, someone who organizes and inventories donations, and someone who supervises projects, based on the size and participation of your staff. Or, you may want everyone to do a little bit of everything together in order to build community and continue to capitalize on an enthusiastic climate. This may work well, especially if there is a small, core group of people involved. All you need is some momentum, and more people will likely come aboard as makerspace takes shape. Having a grade-level representative may help this process.

When you actively demonstrate creativity and flexibility, you are modeling the teaching style you value, helping shift the culture. Introduce makerspace to your staff as a rewarding and desirable experience. Participating in a maker activity, watching a powerful video clip, or going on a site visit can be very motivating for adults as well as for children. Providing opportunities for teachers to take risks boosts morale and builds teams.

Happy, motivated, curious teachers can lead to happy, motivated, curious students. It is very possible for a principal to shape climate, which shapes culture over time. A culture of makerspace hits the philosophical jackpot for positive teaching and learning. Inviting teachers to participate at their comfort level is an important aspect at the beginning of this initiative.

BELIEFS ABOUT LEARNING

While the concept of makerspace might be relatively new, the underlying teaching and learning theories are deeply embedded in our educational history. Makerspace fits in with values associated with Piaget's Constructivist Learning, Renzulli's Enrichment for All, and project-based learning (PBL). Student creativity, a growth mindset, and engaged learning all contribute to a positive makerspace experience.

Makerspace provides opportunities for all students to participate in meaningful, hands-on, problem-solving challenges. Piaget's constructivism theory promotes discovery as the basis of learning. According to Piaget, children go through stages in which they accept ideas they may later discard as wrong. New understandings are developed step-by-step through active participation and involvement (Piaget 1973).

A constructivist approach allows students to take responsibility for their own learning. Students create, then analyze their own questions, and are encouraged to make connections between ideas. They can then use higher-order thinking skills such as predicting, evaluating, and justifying their ideas to others (Brooks and Brooks 1993). In makerspace, we honor Piaget's approach by providing students with opportunities to solve open-ended challenges, providing a wide range of supplies and materials to choose from, and providing time and support to use trial and error in the design process.

Principles of Enrichment for All are based on Joseph Renzulli's Schoolwide Enrichment Model (SEM), which was developed in the 1970s in connection with the National Research Center on the Gifted and Talented at the University of Connecticut. These principles include the understandings that every learner is unique and that students learn more effectively when they are working on a real problem and are enjoying the process.

The major goal of enrichment is to enhance thinking skills through a student's own construction of meaning (Renzulli 1998). Makerspace provides opportunities for all students, regardless of their grades and test scores, to participate in hands-on activities that are based on real-world situations. Makerspace isn't reserved for gifted and talented students—it is truly enrichment for all. Each student will use the supplies and materials provided in a different way; each student will need differing levels of support in terms of motor skills and independent problem solving. Each student will grow as an innovative thinker and will undoubtedly learn new skills and strategies through makerspace opportunities. Some may learn how to use a new tool or technique, others may learn a new math or science concept, and still more students will learn how to share, work collaboratively, be patient, and have confidence in themselves and in others.

Project-based learning is built on the work of Piaget, Dewey, and Montessori, among other education and child development experts. In K–12 education, project-based learning has become a method of teaching that involves rigorous, relevant, hands-on learning. Makerspace can be a hub for PBL in your school. There is some discussion about project-based versus problem-based learning, but the philosophies are very similar.

It is important to distinguish PBL from projects done at the end of a unit of study. PBL is not making a penguin after learning about penguins, or making a poster listing facts that were researched about an important historical figure. In PBL, the project is the *centerpiece* of the lesson where a proposed project is introduced along with open-ended questions that are the driving force for students to investigate and find their own solutions for (Boss 2011).

For example, a PBL assignment can be for a group of students to construct a habitat that would be sustainable for a penguin, requiring students to do research about the animal and its needs, then use supplies and tools in makerspace to create a model home. Another idea would be to have students learn about famous inventors, then make their own invention that solves a problem in their lives, using makerspace to create a prototype. The learning goes hand in hand with the making; one doesn't come before or after the other. Some people suggest adding an *R* to STEAM so it is all about STREAM, the *R* standing for *research*. That coincides well with project- or problem-based learning.

Student creativity, a growth mindset, and engaged learning all contribute to a positive makerspace experience and are inherently constructivist, enriching, and problem based. Teachers can promote, and children can learn, a variety of ways to express their creativity. Staff and students can transition from a fixed mindset to a growth mindset by tinkering and creating, allowing themselves to revise their ideas and revisit their plans. Engaged learning can be developed through activities and discussion in a classroom that promotes a hands-on, minds-on environment.

Some students, and some teachers, consider themselves to be creative, while others do not. There are at least two types of creative people: those whose work leads to big changes in the world, such as architects and famous artists, and those who create to have an effect on their everyday lives, such as flower arrangers and local artisans. Creativity, and making, becomes accessible to us when we realize that our day-to-day activities and projects are realistic, meaningful, and reasonable ways to express ourselves. We don't all have to be Michelangelo to be considered creative (Drapeau 2014).

Opportunities to tinker and invent can lead to excitement, and teachers and students will likely put more effort into making if they believe they are creative. Principals, by encouraging divergent thinking and acknowledging varying types of creativity, can serve as a springboard for others to value their individual type of creativity.

When you believe that your habits, personality, and skills are changeable and are constantly developing, evolving, and in progress, you demonstrate a growth mindset (Dweck 2007). You think to yourself that if you put effort in, you can effect a positive outcome. In makerspace, it is important for students to understand that their ideas, energy, and unique way of viewing the world all contribute to a successful experience.

A growth mindset is contrasted with a fixed mindset, where someone thinks about themselves in an immovable way—you are what you are, and there's nothing you can do to change, so there's no reason to put in effort or try. If a student or teacher has a fixed mindset, makerspace will present challenges since projects require people to take risks, try new things, face less successful attempts, and consider feedback to revise a project. Principals may need to work with staff to provide resources to help students and staff develop a growth mindset so that they place value on effort, leading to successful making.

Student engagement is needed for inventing, tinkering, and creating. Some children are more naturally engaged learners, and others may need a teacher or mentor to help them become engaged. The following traits describe engaged learners: optimistic, persistent, flexible, resilient, and empathetic (Mraz and Hertz 2015). Classroom teachers can embed lessons that promote these traits so that all students have the opportunity to be engaged learners and to acquire new strategies that they can apply in makerspace and in their lives in general.

You can support your teachers by providing articles, video clips, and professional books on these topics so they can facilitate curriculum that explicitly teaches the skills of engaged learning. Some recently published books you may want to peruse include *Launch* by John Spencer and A. J. Juliani and *Sparking Student Creativity* by Patti Drapeau. The website www.mindfulschools.org offers video clips and lesson ideas for teaching mindfulness in elementary schools, which can be applied and adapted to help engage learners.

An administrator's beliefs about learning shape the programs that take place in their school. By valuing makerspace, you are valuing hands-on, project-based, enrichment opportunities for all students. Creativity, a growth mindset, and student engagement all play a role in makerspace, and equipping your staff and students with these skills and strategies will be beneficial in makerspace.

DIVERSE LEARNERS

Diverse learners include students who learn using different modalities, such as being predominantly visual, auditory, or kinesthetic. Diverse learners also include students who learn with varying levels of adult support for academic, social, and emotional needs; those who learn better individually or in a group; and those with varied interests. Principals spend time looking critically at staff and students with an eye on the strengths and needs that will need to be considered as they create a makerspace. Principals can try some of these suggestions and think about how their observations align with their beliefs about learning.

- While you are observing teachers' lessons throughout the year, focus on student learning. Note which activities are engaging and how students respond to a variety of materials. Which students are less engaged, and what may help them become more active learners? Are additional manipulatives needed? Do students need more time to collaborate? Are questions open ended, and do they allow for multiple correct responses?

- Watch students problem solve in the cafeteria and at recess and at other strategic moments such as on field trips or at special events. See their social interactions and fine and gross motor abilities. Observe what students' outside interests are and what they like to play with when they are self-directed.

Through these observations, you may see students teaching each other a skill or strategy or notice enthusiasm for a specific topic, excitement about special materials being used, and other visible signs of engagement. Consider ways to incorporate what you observe into makerspace to ensure diverse materials, projects, and support.

For example, if your students and teachers are excited about ancient civilizations, animal habitats, or extreme weather, you can include projects and supplies that can further their creative investigation of these topics. In makerspace, students can use clay and building materials to make 3D landscape models to observe the effects of weather. They can work in teams to create stop-motion animation videos using apps on tablets or programs on laptops to depict scenes from ancient civilizations. Students can use a variety of materials such as aluminum foil, wooden sticks, straws, and Styrofoam to make a habitat for a real or imaginary animal. Encourage your teachers to try out the materials, programs, and projects in advance so that any concerns are addressed before the students participate in a given activity.

To reach all learners and provide support for all, it is important to have information available to students in many modalities. To provide visual support, it is important to post necessary information or instructions on a chart as well as to have a diagram to hand out, or display a slide on an interactive white board. Clearly label supply bins with the names and photographs of their contents, such as printing the word "rubber band" and including an accompanying illustration.

Consider having instructions available via audio for those who need repetition—you can use a QR (quick response) code that students can scan with a tablet as needed. QR codes can be created using free Internet resources, and they look like a square filled with a black and white pattern. A QR code can include an audio recording of the teacher explaining the directions or a video with clear, step-by-step instructions. Provide a sample of a finished or partially finished project as a reference for those who need additional visual and kinesthetic support. Have some materials available for students to touch and manipulate to assist kinesthetic learners.

You may want to include materials in your makerspace that can be used in many ways rather than just having kits with instructions where everyone makes the same thing. Some ideas to consider are as follows.

- Include a project library with photos and instructions about making many different things so students have choices.
- Have visual reference materials available, organized in something such as a three-ring binder with clear pages that are filled with project ideas accompanied by photographs and instructions. Sample projects can be displayed on a nearby bulletin board or in an electronic database.
- Have a large variety of materials and supplies available that students can select from when making projects as part of their learning experience. Some students are not accustomed to having choice and at first feel stuck and need guidance regarding how to select appropriate supplies.
- Offer real-world problems that need creative solutions, and guide students to prepare to share their projects with authentic audiences.
- Arrange authentic audiences for students to present to, such as small groups of students, teachers, parents, a local organization, or a pen pal via video conferencing. Students can share their idea as a contest entry, with a politician to support a local initiative, or any other person, group, outlet, or publication that will benefit in some way from the students' projects. Be sure to have parents' permission as needed.

You may find that students' problem-solving skills aren't necessarily positively correlated with age or standardized test scores. That is, fifth graders aren't necessarily better at making than kindergarteners, and students with an A academic average don't necessarily have more success in makerspace than those who have difficulty with core subject areas. Students who struggle with traditional academics may have an awareness of the world around them and interact with tools and materials to solve problems very capably. Students who are good athletes may or may not be good at fine-motor activities. Students who struggle in math may be very capable at using supplies to create a solution to a difficult environmental problem. Offering diverse, enriching opportunities to all students can level the proverbial playing field and provide creative experiences for every child.

Diverse learners also need diverse supplies. You may need to select large and small versions of the same or similar items (such as beads, scissors, paper clips, and buttons) and some materials with an obvious use and others that need to be used inventively (paper and crayons versus cardboard tubes). If you have access to an occupational or physical therapist who works with your students, they can be a tremendous resource to you in terms of identifying tools and materials that will be well suited for students with varying fine- and gross-motor needs.

Diverse learners may also include students with medical needs such as allergies or chronic illnesses. When selecting any items for use by or near students, be sure they meet all health and safety requirements, and take any allergies into consideration. For example, if a student has a latex allergy, be vigilant when selecting balloons or other plastic products. Do not repurpose containers that held items with nut products in them, to avoid possible severe allergic reactions. It is suggested that you review all student allergies and special medical situations with the school nurse, keeping makerspace materials and projects in mind. Be aware of which cleaning agents are permitted by your district and local agencies so you can appropriately remedy any spills or situations with approved supplies.

In a makerspace that supports philosophies including enrichment for all and aligns with a project-based, constructivist approach, there are materials, tools, and projects that can be adapted to meet each student's diverse needs so that all learners can work on authentic problems and gain new skills. Principals can informally observe students' problem-solving skills in classes and among grade levels to inform the types of opportunities that they will provide and support in makerspace for all students to enjoy.

THREE
Creating and Cultivating Space

Location is the biggest element in the real estate market, and it is a large factor in classroom designations as well. Finding room for makerspace involves many considerations based on each school's layout, population, foot-traffic patterns, and other individualized factors. To optimize the value of your makerspace, view your school as if you were a location scout and consider a large range of options. You might decide that more than one location is needed, or begin in one location and move to another. Use a current building map or architectural blueprint as your guide. There may be spaces that even the principal doesn't know about.

CREATING SPACE

Creating a makerspace location within your school building is the first step; cultivating the space to become a thriving center of activity comes next. As the building administrator, you know how the various rooms are utilized within your school, what your enrollment numbers are and what enrollment numbers are predicted to be in the near future, and what resources you have available in case any structural changes are needed. Keeping that information in mind, think about the following questions when choosing a location for your makerspace:

- **Student population:** How many students will use makerspace at the same time?

- **Shared location:** Will it be in a space used for other classes or groups?
- **Safety, sanitation, and cyberspace:** Does the location meet all requirements?
- **Supplies:** How and where will materials be made available to students?
- **Storage and furniture:** Where will extra supplies be stored? What furniture will be used?

Makerspace takes up space, plain and simple. How much space you are able to devote to it, and what will be inside the space, depends on your answers to the above questions. Each component will be expanded upon below to help you select a prime location for your students to tinker, invent, explore, and create. You may want to collaborate with your head custodian or facilities office, technology department, a supervisor or director of STEAM content areas, and other building administrators in your district to select the best location. Share any major changes with your central administrators, and ensure any necessary approvals before making a final decision. Be sure that the location of your makerspace appears on any new maps and that your local fire department has an updated version.

STUDENT POPULATION

The size of the space you choose will depend on the maximum number of students who will be using makerspace at the same time. Conversely, if the only space available for makerspace is compact, then the number of students who can use it becomes dependent on the size of the room. Either way, a large or small makerspace can be very successful based on the accessibility of the materials. As a goldfish grows to the size of its tank, be assured that your makerspace will grow to fill the location you select.

At first, you may not believe this, but after your first batch of supplies comes in, and after groups of students use the space and need room to maneuver their supplies and projects, you will immediately see what changes are needed to make the space work to your advantage. You will want to build a loft, tear down walls, and rearrange storage closets. However, even if you only have a rolling cart and a large box, you can have a makerspace.

If you have the option to select any space of your choosing, think about the enrollment in your largest class. Will the room you are considering accommodate that number of students? Consider that you will need furniture—whether it is tables and chairs, stools and counters, or mobile pieces—as well as storage and shelving for materials and projects. You may want to map out how furniture could be arranged in the room, which will help determine how many chairs and tables can fit, which will help estimate the number of students who can be in makerspace at the same time.

Two or more classes might want to collaborate on a project and use makerspace together. Can your location fit that many students? You may want to have a rug or carpet squares available for groups of students to use when they work together. Instead of just chairs, some benches may fit more students into the same space more compactly. Portable surfaces such as clipboards, lap desks, and trays help make seating and furniture arrangements more flexible as well.

If you have a large student population, but a relatively small location to utilize, there are still many creative ways to design a fabulous makerspace. If the room is the right size for a small group of students, then it can be used during recess, before or after school as a club, or with a teacher who takes a few students in there at a time.

If it is big enough to hold materials, but there'd be no room left for students, then your makerspace can be mobile. Portable activity kits can be put together in empty copy-paper boxes or clear plastic containers and made available for teachers to take back to their classrooms to use with students. Suggested project ideas, photos, and directions can be included. Alternatively, a cart can be filled with a variety of supplies in covered containers (such as pipe cleaners, clothespins, cardboard tubes, scissors and tape, foam, yarn, and more), and the cart can be rolled to another location to be used with students.

SHARED LOCATION

Often a classroom is shared by staff such as part-time service or therapy providers, or teachers use the room on different days of the week or at different times of day. Before or after school, rooms are sometimes used for child care, clubs, scout troop meetings, or PTA events. Is the location you are considering for makerspace a room that will be shared? If it is, then you may want to think about storage options, room dividers, a posted schedule, and other ways to delineate who uses the room when, and where various supplies will be kept.

Shared space can be a flourishing makerspace. Depending on if the room is shared based on a schedule or partitioned, there are options for how to manage materials and activities. If you are creating makerspace that teachers and services will share at different times of the day or week from others who use the same room, supplies can be kept out of the way in covered, stacked, labeled containers in a closed, and possibly locked, cabinet in this shared area.

If you partition your makerspace so it can be used for more than one purpose at the same time, traditional vertical room dividers can be used to separate and help designate the part of the room that is makerspace. Functional dividers such as a table and chairs, carpet, or shelving can also be used to visually mark off the area.

You may want to have an alternate plan in place for using the shared makerspace should there be a change or glitch in the schedule, or if room usage needs change. This can include a statement about who has precedence over whom in case of a conflicting event, or can designate an alternate location for makerspace in the event of extenuating circumstances, in an effort to avoid potential problems.

SAFETY, SANITATION, AND CYBERSPACE

A location might look as though it's perfect for makerspace, but it is important to consider many safety and technological aspects before making a final decision. Be sure to check with your district's safety officer to ensure that everything is acceptable, and make any accommodations needed to ensure the well-being of your staff and students. These are just some of the many aspects for you to think about.

Safety

- Is the room handicapped accessible?
- Is it in compliance with all fire code requirements?
- Is there an unobstructed rescue window?
- Will you need a sink for the types of activities you envision taking place?
- Will you be including materials that require an eyewash station?

- Do you have posted procedures in this room in case of an emergency?
- Will you need additional outlets for electrical items so you don't overload circuits?

Sanitation

- Which staff members are responsible for cleaning this area (and how do they feel about glitter)?
- What types of wipes or cleaning agents are allowed to be used on surfaces used by students, and who is allowed to handle those cleaners?
- What responsibility will students and teachers have for keeping the space neat and clean?
- Will you have parent volunteers or student helpers, or another plan to help organize stray materials?

Cyberspace

(Only if you are including technology in your makerspace—which is completely optional.)

- Do you need computer hardware drops?
- Do you need Wifi connectivity?
- Will portable technology items be locked up, and if so, who can access them and how?
- Who is responsible for charging and troubleshooting robotic components, tablets, cameras, and other technology in makerspace?
- What is the plan if technology in makerspace breaks or is missing? (Ozobots and 3D Doodlers can be appealing and delicate.)

Safety, sanitation, and cyberspace considerations are better thought out in advance rather than after you have designated a location for makerspace and then have these issues arise. You will be as prepared as possible for any changes that need to be made, such as having outlets moved, tiles replaced, a window fixed, or other physical-plant problems addressed because you took these issues into consideration at the outset. Consulting with appropriate staff who will be involved in maintaining or using makerspace will help the process go as smoothly as possible.

SUPPLIES

Developing a supply stream will be addressed in an upcoming chapter. As you are considering a location, imagine a number of boxes or bins filled with a variety of supplies that all need to go somewhere. There may also be tools or machines, and technology, if that is part of your plan. You may be imagining twenty small boxes or colorful baskets with neat arrangements of supplies or two hundred large clear bins overflowing with materials—either way your location needs to match the quantity and variety of your supplies, and vice versa.

Selecting a location includes planning for where supplies will be kept. Consider if the room you want has or needs closets, book shelves, cabinets, tables, cubbies, or other furniture that can be used to organize boxes and bins. Think about other locations in your school that may have extra available furniture that you can relocate to this new makerspace, and plan where these items might go. Keep in mind that as you get supplies, as teachers use the space, and as you become further entrenched in makerspace culture, you may want to rearrange, reorganize, and redesign your makerspace; so plan to be flexible.

Supplies can be categorized in a variety of ways, and you may want to organize your makerspace based on categories, sections, or themes. You may want to set up your supplies into centers or stations including some of the following categories:

- Cardboard Construction (toilet paper tubes, empty wrapping paper rolls, shoe boxes, corrugated cardboard, Makedo tools and connectors)
- Textiles (felt, material, foam sheets, buttons, beads, bubble wrap, ribbon, thread, origami paper, wrapping paper, tissue paper, Styrofoam pieces, Velcro, contact paper)
- Tools (scissors, hole punchers, glue, staplers, masking tape, pencils, rulers, tape measures)
- Take-Apart—affectionately called "breakerspace" (screwdrivers and small electronics that can be taken apart to see how they work inside with any cords and glass removed)
- Electricity (Snap Circuits, wires, batteries, clay, conductive tape, aluminum foil, LED bulbs)
- Architecture (Lego, Tinkertoys, wooden blocks, Lincoln Logs, Bristle Blocks, magnetic building sets, K'Nex . . . and possibly a rug or carpet squares to sit on while you build)

- Surprise Supplies (feathers, pipe cleaners, bottle caps, clothespins, wooden craft sticks, stickers, plastic cups, small toys, and anything else you may have, coffee stirrers, paper bags, patterned duct tape, brass fasteners)
- Technology (3D printer, zSpace, Ozobots, tablets, Tiggly, Bloxels, Cubelets, Google glasses, digital cameras, dimensional ink pens, Dot and Dash)

In addition to categorization, there are other decisions to make regarding supplies. Do you envision a large or small variety of supplies being made available to students, and will all supplies be available at all times? You can choose to put out just one category of supplies at a time, such as all architecture items only. Everything else would get stored in a closet or covered temporarily so it isn't used. Or, everything can be out all the time, and students can choose to combine items to create projects. How much space you need, or have, can help guide the amount of supplies you offer at any given time.

STORAGE AND FURNITURE

By now you have likely selected a location that is the right size for the number of students that you foresee using it at the same time; determined if it is a shared location and how you will manage the usage of time and space; considered issues surrounding safety, cleanliness, and technology; and have a vision for where supplies will be kept and the amount of supplies that will be made available at a given time. Storage and furniture will come into play at this point.

You will likely have more supplies on hand than you plan to use, so some items will need to be stored. Extras can be placed in a closet in makerspace, stashed under tables in boxes, or tucked under or behind an open container of the same item. If available, you can use an alternate location, such as another classroom, attic or basement, or a combination of these storage suggestions for extraneous supplies. Clearly label whatever you store with what it is and that it is intended for use in makerspace, to assist with easier accessibility when you need to replenish supplies in the future.

Furniture for makerspace needs to be fluid and flexible. Younger and older students will likely be using the same location so there needs to be furniture that can accommodate their different physical needs. Tables and chairs work well for group projects. Consider which table shapes—round, rectangular, flower, or other shapes—would be most practical for your students and your location.

Storage cubbies on wheels are an asset as you can rearrange the room easily, as needed. Large, low, open shelving provides flexibility for displaying a variety of supplies and tools at eye level for students to use. Many companies promote STEAM furniture, including tool carts, mobile stations, elaborate bins, and charging stations. Get a feel for how your unique room is utilized by classes; you may change the room layout as your school's needs change or as your supply stream changes. Then you will likely change it again, and again, making student-centered improvements each time.

CULTIVATING SPACE

Growing and developing your chosen location is the next step so that makerspace becomes a busy, activity-filled, valuable resource. After it has furniture and supplies in it, you may notice that your makerspace still needs some work so that it is accessible, teacher and student friendly, and dynamic rather than static. Project libraries, reference materials, samples, posters and signage, merchandising and novelties, and grab-and-go projects can enhance your room to keep it interesting, fresh, and enticing.

Project Libraries

A project library is used to store ideas, directions, photographs, and other papers that can inspire or assist students to choose and complete a project. Three-ring binders with clear page protectors are an easy way to create project libraries. You can also use four-by-six photo books that have openings where you slide pictures in, or index card boxes with dividers; or laminate pages, then punch a hole in the top corner and place them together on a metal ring. Project library formats vary just as makerspaces vary—select and develop a system that works best for your school. You can decide who can add to the library—staff, students, or both.

One large project library can be created to contain many ideas using various supplies, or separate smaller project libraries can be made for each type of material. Project ideas sometimes come with the supply itself and can often be downloaded and printed from the supply manufacturer's website or from other Internet sources where ideas are shared. These ideas can then be placed in the corresponding project library.

For example, fuse beads may be a popular item for students to use to learn about pixelation, and each package purchased comes with sample ideas. Illustrations of these ideas can be combined into a project library specifically for fuse beads. You may want to photograph student-work samples to include in the library. Additional directions can be included, and students or staff can add to the library as they find more examples.

Reference Materials

Students and teachers may need to refer to various resources to more fully understand a project or concept. Having reference materials available in makerspace will facilitate their ability to start or complete a project. This can be accomplished with a combination of books, technology tools, blueprints, and diagrams. Reference materials can be displayed throughout makerspace in a variety of ways.

- Designate a bulletin board for schematic drawings, instructions, and illustrations that are needed to set up and work with materials.
- Pictures in frames can be placed near supplies to indicate ways to use them or to illustrate a finished project. For example, you may want to display basic instructions about how to use a loom near a bin full of yarn. Additional ideas can be included in a project library, also kept near the yarn.
- Books that inspire students to be inventive can be kept in makerspace. They can be on a book shelf together or spread out in the room. Some inspiring titles include: *Rosie Revere, Engineer*; *Iggy Peck, Architect*; and *What Do You Do with an Idea?*
- How-to books are an ideal genre to stock in makerspace. These can include books about how to make crafts using recyclable materials, how to use tools, and how to build just about anything. Students can access these books for general ideas or to follow directions specifically.
- Biographies about famous inventors are a nice addition to your reference library. Books about innovative companies that appeal to students are also of high interest among students. Scholastic offers many relevant titles through their book fair reward catalogs that you can acquire using points earned.

- Students can use computers or tablets that are available to research how things work, to find directions for ways to make something, or to search for additional project ideas. Your school will likely have Internet security in place so that student searches are safe, but it is always important to supervise students while they are on the Internet.
- Instruction manuals can be kept with the items they came with for future reference. If you have a sewing machine, circuit set, or other items with moveable parts, it helps to have instructions nearby. If possible, laminate any paperwork for durability. You may want to reproduce directions and have multiple copies available so students can use them for reference as well as to take them back to class or home to complete a project.

Samples

Having a visual model of sample projects on display is helpful to many learners. You can include samples made by adults or students. Samples can be of a finished project and also of a project in progress to show the different steps involved.

Students may be enthusiastic about allowing you to use their projects as samples or may be so excited about what they made that they can't wait to take it home. Photographing projects can help showcase a variety of work without taking up a lot of space. A student might also want to make a sample to be helpful and donate it to makerspace for perpetuity.

When displaying samples, it is important to keep in mind the wide range of student creativity. Highlighting only perfect examples makes it difficult for some students to try a project for fear that theirs won't be as good as the sample. It is important to show a variety of projects that have different attributes. Some may be neater, others may have more outside-the-box ideas, and still others may be more simplistic. This mix will encourage students to take risks and acknowledges individualism.

Posters and Signage

In most classrooms, there are posters and a sign with titles indicating what happens in different areas of the room. Common signage includes the calendar, word wall, writers' corner, and classroom library. In makerspace, it is also important to include posters and signs to indicate which supplies are where and which areas are designated for certain activities.

If you are segmenting your makerspace into a variety of stations, you can add signs to indicate which area is for cardboard construction, breakerspace, architecture, textiles, technology, and other categories. As each makerspace is different, your signage will depend on your setup. You may want to put posters on the wall, hang a sign from the ceiling over that area (if you are allowed to), place picture frames with the name of the station on the related supplies and work surfaces, put tape on the floor as a visual divider, or color code the bins and furniture by section.

If your makerspace is not separated by stations, signs may help indicate where supplies are generally kept and where the resource and project libraries are and to denote storage. Students and teachers may also need space for projects that are under construction, so if possible, plan for an area to store these as well.

You may want to put up posters that explain the engineering and design process including these stages: ask what the problem is, imagine solutions, plan by making a diagram and listing materials, create something, test it out, and modify your project to make it better based on what worked and what didn't. These posters can be store-bought or handmade. The process is cyclic, so having the posters in a circle or indicating movement among and between the stages of the design process would be beneficial. You may want to include students, parents, and art staff to make the posters more of a personalized experience, if time permits.

Merchandising

As a customer, when you walk into stores, you see merchandise displayed in a certain way that attracts your attention, leads you further into the store, and encourages you to spend money on the goods. In makerspace, the students are the customers—it is your role to facilitate the organization of the room and supplies so that it is inviting, leads students to want to explore further and be inspired to put forth energy and expend effort to make, tinker, and create. You can do this alone, with a committee, or by designating other staff or parent volunteers to merchandise your makerspace. You might want to take your cues from stores your students like, such as local toy stores, clothing stores, and candy stores to see what catches their eye. Distinctive display features, amusing string lighting, moving parts, and unexpected items may do the trick.

Many materials and supplies are self-explanatory and can be placed in bins with no other effort or explanation needed. Students will likely know how to use most common items such as cups, yarn, clothespins, wood sticks, crayons, and straws. Students can be inspired to use these items in creative ways by your pointing out sample projects or photos or directing them to project libraries.

Other supplies are more mysterious and may require some clarification. For example, rubber stamps in a bucket labeled "stamps" by themselves may seem to be obvious. However, if you pair the stamps with folded cardstock, colorful paper scraps, decorative scissors, ink pads and a sign that says "Make Cards" students may view the stamps differently and purposefully. Adding "Make Cards for Soldiers, Volunteers, and Birthdays" might be even more helpful.

For some students, the variety of supplies in makerspace can be overwhelming, and they don't know where to begin in order to create a project. You can help them by selecting, in advance, a sampling of about five different supplies. Choose items such as a cardboard tubes, pipe cleaners, bottle caps, Styrofoam peanuts, and wooden sticks and display them together in a box or tray. Put a sign on or near that display asking students to use these preselected materials to invent a new toy, create a new animal, or develop a new kind of transportation. These items will engage students' hands and minds and still offer creative choice but in a way that is more comfortable for them than having a whole room to select supplies from. Then, students can add materials once they have begun their project and gained confidence in their ability to create and make decisions and revise their ideas.

Look around your makerspace and see which supplies you can combine to suggest projects that can be made, or show a variety of samples displayed near an underutilized item to attract student customers. Rearrange some supplies so they are in a prime location to entice students to use them, or remove an item for a while that doesn't seem to get used very much, then bring it back to create excitement.

Novelties and Grab and Go

Items that are unique or interesting capture our attention. Students will be intrigued by tools and supplies that are unusual or special in some way. Throughout the year, consider focusing some makerspace activities around holidays, special events, popular culture such as movie characters, and anything that you can acquire that is new, rare, or different in some way. Cups can be just cups, but when they have cartoon characters on them, they become exciting cups that make hesitant students want to utilize them to create skyscrapers. Students may be more likely to use supplies that they can relate to, that make them feel confident, or that tell a story.

Some students still may not be able to select materials, despite the labeling and merchandising in place, due to varying learning styles. For these students, having a Grab and Go section or bin will be very helpful. Here, place individual projects that are prepackaged and ready to be made. A clear illustration and instructions along with all needed supplies should be included. You may get some donations that would be perfect for the Grab and Go, such as individual seasonal projects, or you can prepare some using supplies on hand.

Creating space is the first obstacle; in order to inspire young makers, you need space that meets the needs of your school. Cultivating that space so that it promotes innovation and creativity is an ongoing responsibility that can turn an ordinary room into an extraordinary initiative.

FOUR
Developing a Supply Stream

Makerspace requires supplies, ranging in complexity from no tech to high tech and from free to expensive and can be in any quantity—from a simple box full of items to a storage room overflowing with materials. There is no official list or set of rules for what needs to be in a makerspace. Yours is unique and will reflect your vision. A supply stream depends on your school's resources, which can vary based on student enrollment, community involvement, budgetary resources, and storage options.

For example, if your school has two hundred students, you may need fewer supplies than if your school enrolls thirty-five hundred students. If you have a large room for makerspace that includes storage areas, you can likely manage more materials than if your makerspace is on a rolling cart. Some supplies are consumable and others are reusable; the quantity of those items may vary based on enrollment or space available. Be assured that no matter how few or how many items you have, or what size space you can use, students will have powerful learning opportunities.

There are many ways to accumulate items for makerspace. Students can bring in household items to donate, grants can be written to acquire funds for items needed, community resources can be used, and special events can be held to bring in supplies. The wider you cast your net, the more variety you will notice in your materials.

Unexpected items may appear, which may inspire you and your students to utilize supplies in new, creative ways. Supplies run out, new materials are needed, and innovative ideas will come your way. If you are solely budgeting for and purchasing all needed items and not relying on donations, then some of the following steps would not be needed; however, the supplies detailed below would still be helpful and relevant. Whether you are using donations, purchasing through your budget, or a combination of both, a steady supply stream is necessary for a well-stocked and motivating space. Being creative, collaborative, and innovative will help you through this ongoing process.

Starting with your own personal ideas and expanding to include the ideas of your teachers, students, and parents will help create a robust cache of supplies. While explaining makerspace to your staff, elicit ideas for supplies to be included. You may also want to ask students what they'd like to have available to use. If you have a parent committee or involved parents, then find out what they suggest as well. By researching makerspace supplies online you will also come across many lists of suggested items. Creating your own list is more powerful than using someone else's. The following suggestions will help you devise a list that is just right for your school's unique makerspace.

HOUSEHOLD ITEMS

Students' sense of ownership is a critical component to their learning. If they feel involved in the process of supplying items for makerspace by bringing in donations, students will be more likely to want to use the items, take risks, and make the connection between their home and school as places where learning occurs. Students in different communities have varying levels of access to items to donate, and it is imperative that we consider what resources are available in our individual communities. To begin the process of making a list of items for suggested donations, you may want to look around your own home, room by room, to see what is easily available for families to donate, and create a list of supplies needed or wanted based on your observations.

- In the kitchen, empty paper towel rolls, plastic bottle caps, zip-close bags, plastic spoons, toothpicks, aluminum foil, sponges, small paper plates, plastic cups, twist ties, and empty egg cartons are all useful. Coffee filters, paper cupcake liners, brown paper lunch bags, disposable aluminum pans, straws, and corks add to the mix. These can become catapults,

robots, fantasy creatures, and animal habitats in the hands of children.
- The bathroom is full of potential supplies. Empty toilet tissue rolls are versatile and the right size for young students, as are empty tissue boxes. Safety pins, small three-ounce bathroom cups, cotton balls, batteries, and cotton ear swabs are some suggestions. These can be used to make cars, helicopters, games, and houses.
- Garages are gold mines for non-consumable makerspace donations. Small screwdrivers, wire cutters, pliers, tape measures, sandpaper, nuts, bolts, screws, washers, wrenches, duct tape, masking tape, painter's tape, clamps or a vice, electrical tape, and wire can be used for so many projects. It is important to check that these are all safe items that meet necessary standards and that all tools will be used under adult supervision.
- Other rooms such as bedrooms, offices, dens, storage spaces, craft corners, living rooms, and basements can be a valuable source of supplies if you are looking carefully and critically. Old board games can be repurposed, especially spinners, dice, and game pieces. Office supplies such as paper clips, rubber bands, brass fasteners, glue, staplers, binder clips, and various kinds of tape are very versatile. Clothespins, yarn, thread, material, stickers, pom-poms, wooden craft sticks, fast-food toys, foam pieces, wrapping paper, marbles, crayons, scissors, markers, colored pencils, lanyard, pipe cleaners, beads, googly eyes, hole punchers, crochet hooks, stuffing or batting, building and interlocking toys, and Ping-Pong balls all add to the variety of supplies available for students to utilize as they create, tinker, and innovate.

Once you have compiled your list of household items that can be donated, you need to develop a plan for requesting these items. You can simply send out a list of everything to every student. This list would include all of the items you noted by going room to room in your home. It might be helpful to organize your list in some way, whether it is alphabetical by supply or categorized by the room it would most likely be found in. Sending home this list will probably bring in a large quantity and variety of supplies if families have access to these items. Prepare for an onslaught of random donations by setting up a donation box labeled "Makerspace" so students can put their items in a designated location. Be ready to have staff and/

or parent volunteers to help you sort and store these items into labeled bins, boxes, or bags.

You might not be ready for a mountain of paper towel rolls and yarn just yet and prefer a more gentle entry to supplying and stocking your makerspace. In that case, there are several strategies you can use to create a gradual supply stream. Divide the supply list by grade level, and, for example, have second graders bring in kitchen items on the list, third graders bring in bathroom items, and so on. Another option is to send the complete list home and ask each child to bring in only one baggie filled with supplies so the donation load is more manageable.

Grants

There are grants available, especially for STEAM projects, which can help add to your supplies. Some grants require that the materials purchased be non-consumable or reusable, so it is important to decide how to best utilize available grant resources. Some grants can be written personally, and some are written on behalf of the school district—carefully note how the grant is awarded and where they money needs to be deposited. Be sure to check with your school business administrator to ensure proper channels and procedures are followed for money or items received. Your teachers may be eligible for different grants than you are as an administrator and parents in the community can also be involved in grant writing on behalf of their child's school. Pool your resources and apply for anything you may be eligible for. If you receive a grant, be sure to thank or otherwise acknowledge the donor.

If your grant is for non-consumables, you may want to order technology items such as robotics, cameras, or tablets. Furniture and storage items are also non-consumable and can be a costly one-time purchase. Toys for building, storage containers, and shared supplies such as scissors, staplers, and hole punchers may seem simplistic but are often heavily used in makerspaces and might be available through a grant. Additionally, you may want to apply for a grant that integrates literacy into makerspace by requesting books such as how-tos, biographies of inventors, and inspiring picture books.

Developing a Supply Stream

COMMUNITY RESOURCES

Book companies, craft companies, local businesses, and hardware stores may be able to donate quantities of supplies to your makerspace if you make a request on behalf of your school. Check with your business administrator to find out what the procedures are in your district for accepting donations, to ensure that all requirements are met. You may need to include the approximate value of the donation as well as provide item descriptions and model numbers; board of education approval may be necessary.

Local businesses that are owned independently have different processes for considering donations from national chains or big box stores. You may be able to bring information written on school or district letterhead to a local business requesting a donation. For a larger company, you most likely would have to send a letter to their central headquarters in addition to approaching a local branch manager or supervisor. Keep in mind that donations from companies, locally or nationally, can take a while to come through, if at all, so consider these items for a future project rather than a right-now project.

There are often businesses nearby that have items to donate but wouldn't generally think of a school as a location to donate to, until they hear about your makerspace. For example, a paint store may have cans of custom colors that they cannot sell, paint stirrers you can use, and extra paint-chip color samples for students to use for projects. A local business may have unused office supplies that they can donate, such as thirty bags of rubber bands or boxes of three-ring binders they no longer use. Shoe stores may have empty shoe boxes, grocery stores may have corrugated cardboard, and plumbers may have extra PVC pipes and pipe insulation. Students can use these items when constructing projects and applying their knowledge of science concepts, such as to create roller coasters, bridges, and other inventions.

An office supply store may have blank CDs that can be used with a balloon and a sports water-bottle top—for hovercrafts. Gathering supplies is a first step—determining what the supplies will be used for comes later. Often, students and teachers will think of innovative uses for found items. Your role is to get the supplies into makerspace so students and staff can be inspired to create and explore.

Talk about your makerspace everywhere you go. You may be surprised at who hears you and what they have to contribute. Parents have diverse hobbies and interests that require a variety of skills and supplies that might become available to use with students. Grandparents have things to donate and are glad they can be put to good use. People have jobs, and second jobs, that you might not know about and have access to items that would be a perfect fit for makerspace. Sometimes just talking about makerspace helps generate new ideas through conversations. Stay open-minded and keep your eyes and ears open for opportunities. You will likely now look at found objects and think, "I can use that in makerspace!"

SPECIAL EVENTS

A steady supply stream goes beyond the initial donation list that served as the starting point for materials. If you are relying on donations, it is important to generate continuing enthusiasm for makerspace and encourage students, teachers, and families to keep makerspace supplies on their radar. This way, donations continue arriving throughout the year and over the course of years to come. There are many ways to accomplish this by capitalizing on, or creating, special events.

Practical times to gather specific donations are connected to naturally occurring events, such as holidays and seasons. Your school may have events planned throughout the year, such as a science night, barbeque, or holiday fair, possibly in partnership with a PTA. If possible, you can add a request to the event's notice for families to bring a specific item to donate at that event that can be used in makerspace. This can become a tradition, and families will start to look forward to seeing what is needed or wanted next.

In the fall, you may find that families are enthusiastic about sending in donations, since the majority of the school year lies ahead. This would be a good time to send home a longer list of desired supplies. Many people use a large quantity of wrapping paper and have empty cardboard rolls that they either throw out or recycle in December. Also at this time of year, there are often unused or extra craft supplies. You can send a message home to parents that makerspace can put these items to good use—be prepared with a tall cardboard box or container to gather all of the empty wrapping paper rolls that will come in with students.

Color-themed donations are another option. In February, there are often lots of heart-shaped craft supplies and boxes; baking items with hearts; red, pink, and white yarn and fabric; and other odds and ends that can be repurposed. You can send a request home to send these items to school for use in makerspace with a Color of the Day (or "of the week" or "of the month") donation by asking families to send in supplies that are red, white, pink, purple, and so on. In March, you may want to request green and yellow supplies. October and November might be good times to request orange and brown items. You might get felt, doilies, foam, fabric, buttons, thread, and feathers.

In April, families may celebrate holidays and/or do general spring cleaning. This is an opportunity to gather seasonal supplies such as egg cartons, fake grass, plastic eggs, colorful plastic utensils, and cups, stickers, craft items, and small toys. It is a good idea to send a notice home in advance so families can plan to put aside these items rather than sending a note home right after they have disposed of these supplies. You may want to indicate that containers that held food items are not safe for makerspace if you are concerned about contact, ingestion, or airborne allergies. You can check with your school nurse to see if this should be considered.

At the end of the school year, students often bring home everything that was in their desk, including well-worn school supplies. Items such as scissors and rulers can be repurposed in makerspace if families aren't saving them for the upcoming school year. As teachers send supplies home with students, you can include a note requesting old supply donations and leave a box labeled for these items. The beginning of the school year is also a good time to request donations of crayons, glue, colored pencils, and markers. As parents are purchasing these items on sale for their children, they may be able to buy an extra item to donate to makerspace. Shoe boxes are also more available as parents get their children new shoes in preparation for the new school year. These boxes can be used for various projects throughout the school year in makerspace, as well as for supply storage.

A Donation of the Day or Donation of the Month program is an option where you send a makerspace calendar home with students that lists specific household items that will be collected and when. This can be done in many different ways. You can have a Maker Monday, where every Monday all year, a new item to be donated is listed. Or, for Maker Month, select any month of the year—preferably one that doesn't have a lot of other events or holidays occurring—and list a different item to be collected each day throughout the month.

Another idea is to have one item highlighted each month, and each month select one newly needed supply to be donated. If you have an especially competitive school, in a friendly way, you can turn the donations into a contest where the grade with the most plastic bottle caps donated gets to use them first, for example. If there are other schools in your district with makerspaces, you may want to share supplies if you have an abundance of something the other school needs, and vice versa. Sometimes there really is such a thing as too many toilet tissue rolls.

After sending out a donation request to families, whether on paper or electronically, follow up by thanking everyone in general for the materials and supplies. Take photos of students using the items, or photos of the sheer quantity of supplies collected, in order to show the impact of everyone's generosity. As you find new projects for students to create in makerspace, you will likely have a wish list of supplies. Keep this list available so that when people ask what you need, or if a grant becomes available, you are prepared. We found that stickers that look like eyes, marbles, duct tape, and clothespins are very well used by students.

The quantity of supplies that you can manage will depend on how much space you have available. Keep in mind that the quantity of supplies does not correlate to the quality of the creative experience. A makerspace can be as small as a tiny box filled with a couple of toothpicks, rubber bands, paper clips, a pipe cleaner, a foam peanut, a coffee stirrer, and a clothespin, and a student can create an infinite number of projects with a small amount of supplies in a small space. This micro-mini-makerspace can be challenging and fun.

Conversely, a large room filled with buckets and buckets of supplies can be overwhelming and sit idle if students and staff aren't inspired to use it creatively. The combination of available supplies in any quantity along with innovative ideas is what helps a makerspace succeed. Assessing what you need and accessing the supplies is a big undertaking. Having students and families contribute to this shared learning environment is a valuable experience for all.

FIVE
Scheduling, Staffing, and Professional Development

Preparing to implement makerspace involves administrative considerations such as scheduling, staffing, and effective professional development. This chapter includes strategies and suggestions that may help guide you through the additional logistics involved when implementing your unique makerspace experience. For a comprehensive guide, check out *Makerspace Playbook* (Hlubinka et al. 2013), available to view, download, and print as a PDF. It is important to begin by listening to teachers and students about their needs while taking a critical look at scheduling, staffing, and content area curriculum. Data from these encounters can then be used to inform ongoing professional development, leading to a successful makerspace culture for your staff and students.

LISTENING TO TEACHERS

Teachers know their students best and are on the front lines when it comes to implementing new programs. Spend time with teachers individually, by grade level, or as a complete faculty. This can be done formally or informally. Ask questions in person, or use a survey on paper or online using a site such as Survey Monkey, to gather candid information. Some possible questions include:

- What would you do differently in your curriculum if there were no mandated tests?

- What would you do if you had extra free time with your students?
- How would you spend money if you were awarded a grant?
- What would you like to learn more about?
- If we could bring a new program to our school, what would you want it to be?

Write down what teachers say or collect surveys, and read them thoroughly. You will then be able to notice patterns in teachers' responses based on the words you see most often. These responses will likely relate to resources such as time and money, or be connected to stressors such as external pressure and parent involvement, among other concepts. This is the data you will use to plan professional development about makerspace. Some practical ideas to guide you in this process are discussed below.

LISTENING TO STUDENTS

Designing makerspace around students' interests is one of the keys to engaging teaching and learning opportunities (Kurti 2014). Even our youngest learners in kindergarten can express what they like, what they want to do, and what they want to become. It is our job as lead learners to actively listen to gather information about which student-centered resources to include in makerspace. Here are various approaches that can be used independently or in any combination:

- Watch students play during recess, and see what they gravitate toward. You may see them enjoy drawing, building with connecting blocks, playing games, or using their imaginations in other ways.
- Listen in on their conversations with peers during lunchtime. Hear what they do at home, on the weekends, what they collect, what activities they are involved in and passionate about.
- Observe students in their classrooms and special areas such as art, music, physical education, computers, and library. Listen to what they are excited about. See how they interact with each other.
- Talk with students about what they would choose to do in school if they had a free day or free time to do something they enjoy.

- Survey students about what they want to be when they grow up, and think about resources and experiences makerspace can provide that can help students build skills toward these dreams and goals.

Keep lists of students' ideas and interests. You may want to organize this information by grade level or sort it in a way that will help you determine what materials and quantities you need available for which projects.

SCHEDULING

Students need time to create, invent, tinker, and problem solve. Some projects can be completed in fifteen minutes; others can take an hour, or even days. Scheduling time in makerspace depends on the master schedule and available staff, along with the resources and supplies you have available.

Makerspace can be scheduled creatively. You may want to begin by opening makerspace before or after school, as a club, or during lunch and recess. You can work with the special-area teachers such as in art, music, computers, or library to embed makerspace during part of their class time since it incorporates those curriculum standards.

Depending on the size of the school, each class can go for a period once per week or per cycle with their classroom teacher, a STEAM teacher, or other staff member. Alternatively, you may want to focus on one or two grade levels at a time and schedule double periods for those classes in makerspace. Later in the year, you can focus on other grade levels. In this way, classes can work on extended projects, and needed resources can be supplied.

You may want to start scheduling by posting a blank monthly calendar for teachers to sign up for time in makerspace. That way, makerspace is available when they are ready, willing, and able to take their classes in. Save the monthly calendars as data. These can be used to inform future makerspace scheduling based on which grade levels and teachers used it, at what times of day, during which months of the year. The classroom teacher can facilitate their class there, or they may want parent volunteers or support staff to assist to help the session go smoothly. Staffing considerations are offered here to assist you so that you include enough support for teachers and students.

STAFFING

Staffing makerspace can range from very easy to very difficult. It can be done with any amount of resources and may take a bit of outside-the-box planning. All teacher and support staff contracts need to be considered to ensure adequate supervision for students and at the same time follow rules for preparation time required for faculty. Your staffing situation will depend on the role makerspace plays in your school. You may need one teacher there all the time if it is a regularly scheduled class, or you may piece it together with varying staff members if it is more fluid. Some possible staffing options are as follows:

- Propose a maker club for the upcoming school year so an advisor's stipend can be included in the budget.
- Parent volunteers are a great way to have additional adult assistance in makerspace, as long as there is still a certified teacher who is ultimately supervising students.
- The PTA or similar parent group may want to take on makerspace as a committee they solicit volunteers for.
- Make it a duty period for interested staff, if allowed.
- Have a permanent or bench substitute available to assist in makerspace at times.
- Staff makerspace yourself or with the help of any additional building administrators, if you are privileged to have any, and open it during students' lunchtime and recess. That's how we began.
- Involve department supervisors or chairpersons in the math, science, technology, art, and music areas, who may have flexible schedules to staff makerspace. They can also guide STEAM activities.
- If a special-area or academic-intervention support teacher has open space in their schedule, they can staff makerspace during that time.

Various teachers supporting makerspace add diverse perspectives and skill sets, enhancing the initiative. There can be a logbook available to communicate any suggestions or concerns among staff. Available teachers can take charge of one grade level each for consistency, if possible. Or they can lead one makerspace unit of study if their classes change each marking period or semester, based on master scheduling. Any way you staff it, the most important idea is for makerspace to be as open and available as possible for students.

CONTENT AREA CURRICULUM

Makerspace provides students opportunities to engage in self-directed, real-world, cross-curricular projects. They develop twenty-first-century skills by designing, testing, and manipulating objects and hypotheses. Creations in makerspace involve reading, math, science, writing, art, social studies, character education, music, social skills, and technology, leaving no subject behind. Makerspace provides an informal opportunity for differentiation and choice and a way for students to see how they can make a difference in the world through new ideas. It also levels the playing field for learners of varying academic abilities and backgrounds (Fleming 2015).

Administrators need to work with classroom teachers to take a critical look at content area curriculum to see how makerspace can be a natural fit, rather than being seen as an additional subject. Some units of study may need updating or reimagining, and inviting teachers to use makerspace to enhance their existing curriculum turns makerspace into a value-added destination. Creating or reviewing curriculum maps will show which grades teach which subjects and when. There may be a unit that is taught in several grade levels, but doesn't have to be, based on state standards. In that case, one grade level becomes open to a new unit, and makerspace can fill that opening. There may be a project used at the culmination of a unit that can be replaced with one that uses makerspace resources to include more twenty-first-century skills.

After you look critically at major units of study, you may decide to add makerspace activities. Some ideas include ending a study of famous inventors by having students make a prototype of their invention, having students make a stop-motion video to show what they know about a novel, or having them design a fantasy bedroom or skate park in a shoebox using math concepts like area and perimeter. There are many websites and articles you can use to find grade-appropriate, content-specific STEAM activities by searching the Internet using terms such as *makerspace* or *activities* and the grade or content area you are interested in. Professional development time can then be used for evaluating projects for use with students.

PROFESSIONAL DEVELOPMENT

Teachers and students generally learn when an activity is enjoyable and engaging. It is necessary to craft professional development for teachers that meet these criteria. Staff buy-in is crucial to the ongoing success of a maker culture in school, where risk taking and creative problem solving are valued and encouraged. Makerspace is a dynamic place and changes often with new supplies and activities. Getting teachers into the makerspace mindset is the first step.

As an administrator, it is important to assess where your teachers are on the continuum of being ready for change. Makerspace is most likely a big transition for all, as it involves students making a creative mess, encourages working noise, and yields unpredictable projects. Easing into makerspace will help teachers learn more about it, find ways it can work best for them and their students, work with mentor colleagues, and dive in when they are ready.

Talking to teachers and sharing your own interest and excitement about makerspace is a positive first step. Sharing professional books, articles, and websites about the maker movement is a suggested follow-up activity. Teachers can then be invited to discuss the article at a faculty meeting or in a collegial circle, for those who are interested.

Involving teachers in maker activities among peers comes next. Select a hands-on challenge, activity, or problem for staff to do as a grade level or in small groups with the full faculty. Try the activity ahead of time to be sure it works, and be sure that all necessary supplies are available.

Take photos, if allowed, of your staff being true makers. Post the pictures in the faculty room or on a bulletin board in makerspace. If you are on Twitter, tweet about it! Then, at a later date, do this again with a different activity. Fairytale STEM activities work wonderfully, such as having a small group of teachers make a bridge for the gingerbread man to cross the river while another group makes a parachute for a princess to use to escape from a tower or castle. Provide teachers with information about the activity so they can do it with their students if they choose.

Some teachers may emerge as mentors, showing a particular interest in makerspace. Involve these teachers in additional professional development such as by enabling them to attend workshops or joining you on site visits to other makerspaces. All teachers should continue to receive professional development tailored to their readiness levels. Additional options include:

- Pair teachers and classes to participate in makerspace together, possibly putting an upper grade with a lower grade. Activities can be thematic, related to an upcoming holiday, or can be intended to give to others to make the world a better place. Teachers can serve as support for each other during the early stages of making.
- Share a PowerPoint or TED talk about makerspace with staff that they can watch on their own. Having some choice in when and where to learn often encourages participation. Sharing a website of the week or month also promotes independent follow-up. Some prominent sites include Maker Camp, Exploratorium, Make, and Sylvia's Super Awesome Maker Show.
- Continuously let teachers know about upcoming maker movement activities that are happening locally that they may want to attend with their families. Local libraries, science museums, bookstores, craft stores, toy stores, and hardware stores often have maker activities for children on weekends. Often when teachers' children or family members are involved in something they enjoy, those staff members will be enthusiastic about emulating that valued outside experience in school with their students.
- Offer to take a teacher's class to makerspace with him or her, and model a lesson that fits in with the curriculum so the teacher can participate in an activity while not yet having to take ultimate responsibility for it.
- Be involved in makerspace personally. Join teachers while they are there with their students so you can be a resource for them. Ask teachers, and students, what they want to learn next and what supplies and resources they'd like to see in makerspace in the near future.
- Encourage teachers to bring in activities they find that are appropriate for their students. Create a way for teachers to share ideas with each other such as a bulletin board or a project library in a binder or copy and distribute ideas in teacher mailboxes or at an upcoming meeting.

Makerspace will flourish in your school as you lead an environment that encourages risk taking, flexibility, and resourcefulness. Just as each school's makerspace will have different material resources, each has unique scheduling and staffing needs to be met, along with varying levels of teacher readiness. Teachers will be intrigued by ideas and will feel supported by varying kinds of professional development and equipped and excited to implement activities. Students will beam with confidence as they become makers.

SIX
Budget and Branding

Getting makerspace up and running involves allocating space, acquiring supplies, and developing professional capacity. Keeping makerspace going involves planning as it relates to budget and branding. An elementary school principal anticipates being involved in the budget process for the school in general, and the needs of makerspace can be embedded in your school-wide budget. Branding may be a new area to venture into as it relates to expanding your makerspace and can involve public relations, strategic marketing, and a bit of event planning. Ideas to consider are presented here to help you with this process.

BUDGET

As you are involved in the budget process for your school regarding general staffing, materials and supplies, textbooks, furniture and equipment, and facilities, plan ahead to ensure that makerspace continues to grow and evolve for all students. Understand any guidelines from central administration regarding purchasing requirements, sole vendors, and bid requirements to help the budget process go more smoothly, as often STEAM and makerspace items are sold by companies that are newer to the school market.

There are many companies that are marketing STEAM and makerspace products as kits, à la carte, and in boxed programs. Before purchasing any of them, if at all, be sure to research what they have to offer in terms of consumable and reusable items. You may find that the price tag is hefty for disposable supplies that you can acquire more economically. Directions for how to make the project may be available online at no additional cost.

Other companies are encouraging educators to purchase their STEAM-specific furniture. You may find that you already have basic furniture that will suffice. You can put off purchasing specific pieces until your makerspace has been in existence for a while and you have a better feel for what your space, and students, truly need. Or, you may feel better purchasing the kits and furniture so that it is all inclusive and ready to go as soon as the box is opened. Either way, be sure to budget for replenishing items as needed, and to allocate space and storage accordingly.

Budget season brings a lot of mail, especially catalogs, to school administrators. It is tempting to go through brochures and purchase large quantities of items to be sure that you have enough for all of your students, and to buy the latest and greatest robots so you are on trend. Go slowly. Think through which grade levels will likely use a specific item, and start there. You can always order more as needed. That way, if the item or project doesn't go as planned, you don't have buyer's remorse, and you'll still have funds left to purchase something different.

There will always be a newer tablet, a more exciting robot, and more companies soliciting new STEAM products. You can't buy it all, nor do our students need it all. Teachers can't be expected to know how to use every machine or gadget. Taking it slowly will help ease everyone into the maker philosophy of tinkering, creating, and taking risks without feeling worried or burdened. When developing your budget, curb your enthusiasm while planning for an exciting future.

STAFFING

Every school district determines its staffing needs in a different way. If you are able to recommend that a full-time teacher be available for makerspace, or for a STEAM program in general, that's a wonderful opportunity to add staff to develop the program. This may not be possible in your district, so budgeting for staff may require some creative twists and turns.

If a full-time teacher is not an option, possibly a part-time teacher can be recommended to be included in the budget, or a shared staff member can be utilized. Depending on how many students and classes you have, a part-time or shared teacher can work with each class on a rotating basis each week or over the course of the school year. If the staff member is shared with other schools, a schedule can be worked out so that each school gets what they need.

If adding a teacher to the budget is not an option, consider which staff members you currently have available and how they can be used to facilitate makerspace. If special-area teachers have open periods or duty periods, they might be able to spend their time in makerspace either instructing or as a second pair of hands if another teacher brings his or her class there. There might be times during the year when certain grade levels go on trips or are involved in testing, and the special-area teachers can use that time to integrate makerspace into their curriculum with the remaining grade levels.

You may be able to staff makerspace with a teacher's aide who works under the supervision of the classroom teachers. Alternatively, you may be able to budget for clerical or technology department staff to assist with the electronic and Internet-connected components while students are learning in makerspace.

If additional staff is not an option at this point in time, you may be able to have in-school field trips where a local science or engineering organization comes in to work with your students in an assembly or workshop-style visit. This may be something you can include in your budget, or it may be an activity that the PTA can sponsor.

MATERIALS AND SUPPLIES

Budgeting for materials and supplies for makerspace requires patience, research, and restraint. There are so many products to choose from, and with companies online as well as in print, it can become overwhelming to sort through what is right for your school. Taking the time to organize your ideas, plan projects, and inventory your current supplies will help guide you toward what you need to order. You might want to create a curriculum binder, idea map, or other graphic organizer to track what products and projects you are planning for the upcoming year in makerspace, by grade level, in order to manage the materials and supplies you have and that you are going to budget for and purchase. As the supplies come in, you can then allocate them for a certain project and put materials together in a coherent package, labeled and ready to be used.

Often, the budget preparation process begins almost a year before the term the money is intended for—budgeting in November for the next September's school year—which can make it more challenging to anticipate what your needs will be a year in advance. If you are able to budget a placeholder amount of money for makerspace items in general, that would be ideal. That way, you have almost a year to select what specific supplies to purchase. If you need to specify what you will purchase far ahead of time, you may want to include teachers' input to determine what is working and what is needed.

One way to budget for makerspace supplies is per student, as a starting point. For example, if you believe that $10 per student for makerspace items is the right amount for your school, and you have four hundred students, then you'd budget $4,000 for supplies. You may want $3,000 to be consumable materials, and $1,000 to be nonconsumable items, or any proportion that is right for your school's financial situation.

Consider what items will be donated, if you are accepting donations, when selecting items to purchase. If you budget per grade level, you may want to plan for $500 per grade level, times six grade levels if your school is K–5 for instance, totaling $3,000 in consumables. Each grade level might then choose what they need to fit their curriculum if they are looking for boxed programs, or they may combine their resources with another grade level to share supplies.

Before finalizing your budget or buying anything, price out everything you are interested in for makerspace. You may find, based on pricing alone, that you can get more or less of the materials and supplies than you originally planned. Take into account shipping costs, as well as any state contract savings or quantity discounts, when figuring actual costs. If you are budgeting a year ahead, plan for an increase in prices and know that there is the possibility that not all products that are available now will also be available a year from now, so have some backup products or companies in mind, too.

TEXTBOOKS

In makerspace, books are important reference materials for students as well as for staff. The requirements for what is and isn't considered a textbook vary by district. Determine what is considered a textbook by consulting your business administrator so you can plan and budget accordingly. Textbooks may or may not include paperbacks, workbooks that are consumable, text sets, guided reading books, and other items. If these books aren't considered textbooks by your district, you may want to allocate money for makerspace books in your materials and supplies budget.

Books that include instructions about how to make projects or how things work are valuable resources for a makerspace library. Your school's librarian or local public librarian can help you select books, or a series of books, that would be a good fit for your students. You may want to budget for multiple copies of texts that you anticipate being popular so that several students can read the same book at the same time.

Inspiring biographies of inventors are helpful to have available in makerspace. Students will have the opportunity to understand that famous inventors often didn't succeed right away but persevered and tried new strategies, as we want our students to do. Consider budgeting for and purchasing biographies not just of the standards like Einstein and Edison, but also of modern, young inventors from around the world. *Brainstorm!: The Stories of Twenty American Kid Inventors* by Tom Tucker and Richard Loehle is one example. Books about actual inventions, especially ones that students use, are intriguing, as are books about careers involving creativity and engineering.

Balance fiction and nonfiction when selecting texts for makerspace because different students respond to varying genres. There are many fictional stories about inventing and generating ideas that provide information but are ultimately entertaining. Mac Barnett's *Extra Yarn*; Peter Reynolds's *Ish* and *The Dot*; and the many titles by Andrea Beatty, including *Ada Twist, Scientist*, are among my favorites. Having these books available in makerspace can serve as a springboard for students and teachers to have conversations, share ideas, and plan projects. It is suggested that you order multiple copies of these texts as well.

FURNITURE AND EQUIPMENT

Makerspace can be anywhere from no tech to high tech, and your decisions within the furniture and equipment budget will help guide which way your makerspace leans at this point in time. You can always start at no tech to low tech and add more high-tech items over time by setting aside money for them and purchasing them later in the year, or by planning for and purchasing these items in subsequent years—or not at all. There are no rules about technology or furniture that does or does not have to be in makerspace. Your school's needs and resources along with your vision and goals guide what will be included.

High schools and middle schools often have more advanced equipment, tools, and electronics than an elementary school in their makerspace. Older students can work more independently than younger students and are allowed to use more involved machinery than younger students. That said, there are many tools and electronics that are appropriate for an elementary school makerspace.

Robots that teach basic programming are made specifically for younger students. You can buy anywhere from one of each type of robot to a class set, and more. You can buy a few of each kind, then see what is needed before deciding to make an additional purchase. Tablets and digital cameras are equipment that young students can use for stop-motion animation, green screen productions, and making music.

Back-to-basics equipment such as a sewing machine, button maker, and bookbinding machine help students learn about steps in a process and enjoy the satisfaction of creating a finished product. Students can tinker as they learn to follow instructions and use new tools, which will guide them up the pathway to creating their own more complex projects that solve real-world problems (Bevan, Petrich, and Wilkinson 2014/2015).

Having an interactive whiteboard, document camera, and desktop computers is a valuable addition to your makerspace. These equipment options allow a whole class to experience a STEAM opportunity together. If these aren't available, possibly a laptop, projector, and screen would be very beneficial and facilitate whole-class learning.

Furniture can use a large amount of your budget, but generally is a one-time purchase with refurbishing as needed. Your makerspace will need tables and chairs, for which there are many options. Tables can have a dry-erase surface, a chalkboard surface, an interlocking-block surface, a magnetic surface, or a regular wooden surface and come in a range of shapes. You can purchase tables premade with these surfaces, or you can do it yourself with special adhesives or paint.

Chairs can be standard student chairs, stools, large exercise balls, benches, or beanbags. Or, you can have tall tables or stand-up desks and no chairs, which are shown to benefit some students who prefer not to sit while working because they work better standing. The options are infinite. You can have a combination of stand-up and sit-down tables, too. Only you know what is right for your building.

Start with what you already have on hand, then add to it as your makerspace grows, as you see how it is being used and what is needed. In addition to formal seating, you may want a carpet or carpet squares on the floor for students to sit on when they use objects and toys for building and architecture.

Storage is another item to budget for that is often considered either furniture or equipment. Each supply needs to be kept in a storage container, and storage containers being used need to be kept in an accessible storage unit. Additionally, extra supplies and materials not currently being used need to be stored somewhere. Start by using whatever you have on hand, then budget for storage that is consistent throughout your makerspace. If you are starting with assorted bins and baskets, budget for clear bins that are the right size for your space. They are costly but are a one-time purchase that will help facilitate students and teachers using materials.

Decide how much furniture you will need for storage of the supplies in bins depending on whether the bins will be kept on shelves in bookcases, laid out on tables, or kept in a cubby-style storage unit. Budget for any needed storage furniture. Consider buying furniture on wheels, as you may want to reorganize or redesign your makerspace in the future, and having furniture on wheels makes it so much easier to move things—especially when they are full of supplies. Think about how tall you want the furniture to be, and determine whether it needs to be secured to a wall for safety. You may also want to purchase a mobile cart so makerspace can be "on the go" if needed for a specific project, class, or time frame. They make carts with great storage and creative compartments that are makerspace friendly.

If you will have supplies that you aren't using right away, plan for where they will be stored. If you have closets or other areas in makerspace or nearby that are available, you may not need to budget for additional storage. If not, you may want to purchase a large metal, shelved cabinet as a place to store extra supplies. In the meantime, you can use copy-paper boxes or other sturdy containers, clearly labeled, to house your additional materials. Budget for a little more usable storage than you think you need—hopefully you will have a large amount of supplies that will be made available to students, and you will need more shelving or cubbies very soon.

FACILITIES

If you need construction done in order to create a room for makerspace, such as moving walls, doors, windows, heat, lighting, and other electrical or plumbing work, that would need to be discussed with your director of facilities, and costs would need to be budgeted for. If you have a room already, makerspace is a place where there is a lot of activity, and often that leads to the potential for a slight . . . mess. In terms of the facilities budget, plan for a supply of paper towels, chemical-free wipes, a broom and dustpans, and garbage pails and bags dedicated to this venture.

Keep in mind that makerspace can happen on a zero budget—donations of supplies and whatever room, furniture, and containers you have on hand are more than enough to start with. Principals can meet with students before school, at lunch, and at recess in a makeshift space, so no additional staff are needed if none are available. This is how the author's makerspace started, and yours can, too. Anything you can add through the budget is an opportunity to develop makerspace into your ideal experience for students.

BRANDING

Businesses advertise themselves to the public by promoting their brand to attract customers and increase capital. As principal, in addition to the many hats you already wear, you are now also the head of publicity for your makerspace to attract interest and increase participation and innovation. Using public relations opportunities, marketing strategies, and event planning, you will be able to promote your own brand of makerspace. Be sure that you have parent/guardian permission for any photographs, videos, or statements that involve students, and adhere to your district's policies regarding publishing student photos with identifying information when publicizing your makerspace.

PUBLIC RELATIONS

Many school districts work with a public relations firm to some extent. Find out if your district already has a partnership with a public relations company, and use some of your school's allotted print, video, and text quota largely to promote makerspace. You can include students working on projects, talking about their innovations, and explaining or displaying finished products, and offer an overview of makerspace resources available. Highlight willing teachers, parents, and staff and community members who were integral to helping makerspace become a reality.

If you do not work with a public relations firm, there are likely many media outlets available to you within your town, district, or even within your school that can feature your makerspace. Contact local media outlets such as a newspaper, radio, or television station to see if they would be able to feature your makerspace.

Television stations often look to highlight innovation in education, local papers like to feature holiday or thematic events, and radio stations can interview students. Within your district or school, you may have a student newspaper that can include makerspace articles, a student-run radio or video production that can feature makers, or a website where you can upload photos and video clips about makerspace that can be shared with the larger school community.

MARKETING STRATEGIES

The same way that makerspaces can be anywhere from no tech to high tech, your marketing strategy for promoting makerspace can also run the gamut from paper products to cyberspace resources. Social media and print materials offer a wide range of opportunities to share what your students are doing. Including students in the marketing process makes the connection from school learning to real-world experiences.

Social media is a popular venue for publicizing and promoting makerspaces. You can create a blog, use Twitter, a protected YouTube channel, Remind, or many other applications to share student work, upcoming events, and supply requests. Work closely with your district technology department to ensure that the platforms you are using are safe for students to use and view. You may prefer to select apps where you can post a photo or video, which would not be available for public comment to ensure an additional level of decorum and security. You can research what other makerspaces are sharing by typing "makerspace" into the search window of whichever platform you are using in order to gauge what is just right for you.

Include printed materials when branding your makerspace. Parents and students do enjoy seeing their efforts in tangible formats, besides via technology. It is important to be mindful that not all families have equal access to technology, so putting information in all students' hands to share with their parents and guardians is vital. Here are some suggested ideas:

- You can create, or students can create, a newsletter about makerspace and send it home so that families can see the engineering and innovating that takes place.
- Post photographs on a centrally located bulletin board inside your school so that parents can peek at what their children are working on and so students can see themselves and take pride in their efforts.
- Include links to electronic resources such as high-interest websites and apps, and even utilize QR codes to share information in newsletters and on bulletin boards, providing a link between technology and paper documents.

Student engagement is generally high when they are involved in makerspace activities. Capitalize on this by involving students in promoting makerspace. They can create posters to display around the school, make labels for the bins and baskets of supplies, and suggest projects that can be done in makerspace.

Involve your art and music staff to work with students to create a logo and a jingle. Students can work together, or one logo can be selected as part of a contest. This logo can then be made into a sign or banner to be used in makerspace, included on labels for supplies and projects, appear on newsletters, and be made into notepads for students to use to plan their projects.

The PTA might want to become involved and sell T-shirts with the winning makerspace logo for upcoming events, as a fundraiser and to help generate enthusiasm and publicity for this endeavor. A creative jingle can be played over the public address system, included on videos and in other promotional materials to add a layer of audio excitement to the makerspace experience.

EVENT PLANNING

Part of branding your makerspace may involve public events. This can be done in a variety of ways such as having a ribbon cutting when you first open makerspace, offering tours during Back to School Night or parent-teacher conferences, or developing a fair where students and their families come to school and are involved in hands-on projects. You can choose to have one type of event one year, and expand to an additional event the following year, and so on. Having a core group of teachers, parents, and other staff and community members enthusiastically involved helps make events successful so that ideas, as well as the workload, can be shared.

Creatively incorporate your school's mascot, motto, or mission statement into your makerspace branding, especially at public events. This will help to unify your initiative, develop a theme, and organize your plans and materials while combining STEAM with school spirit.

Budget and branding may be a new area for a principal to develop expertise in, but it will enable you to take a critical look at the overall makerspace experience.

Being able to plan for and fund the initiative, and seeing your efforts reflected in student participation that appears in print and photographs, provides an opportunity for you to reflect on your role as the facilitator for makerspace. The results of your reflection will guide the overall direction you'd like this initiative to take going forward. You might be able to transfer your new branding skills to other projects or arenas you are involved in to benefit additional programs.

SEVEN

Assessment

Makerspace is a dynamic environment that, in order to benefit students, needs to continuously evolve to keep up with changes that occur within a school setting. As the school leader, by assessing makerspace in various ways, you will be prepared to make adjustments, both big and small, to keep this initiative relevant and exciting. These suggestions will guide you in deciding what to consider assessing and how often, help you select formal and/or informal tools, and offer ideas for actions to take based on your assessment results.

Makerspace has many moving parts that need to be reviewed in order to continue to succeed. You've worked hard to select, purchase, and organize supplies. Supplies now need to be assessed, along with the budget, so you can adjust your financial resources as needed. You've created a schedule for who uses makerspace and when, so scheduling, staffing, and overall usage of makerspace needs to be assessed so you can best utilize your personnel. Professional development (PD) has been planned and offered in order for teachers to use makerspace, so the effectiveness of that PD needs to be assessed in order for growth to continue.

Student learning in makerspace needs your consideration and can't be taken for granted. Community involvement is another area to assess, along with your own professional growth as it relates to makerspace. There are many formal and informal ways to do this, and the results of these assessments will help you reflect on your initiative and make improvements that will benefit staff and students.

Your school district likely has an assessment calendar where students get report cards or progress reports several times per year, and you probably have other data checkpoints throughout the year for state or national tests that are administered. Think about a schedule for assessing makerspace and determine if you want to assess monthly, quarterly, or as needed. Since there are many qualities to assess, you may want to spread your assessment plans out over the course of the school year. Do you prefer formal techniques, such as lists and numerical data, or informal assessment techniques, such as conversations, photographs, and anecdotal notes, or a combination of the two? Choose what works best for you, and use those selected techniques across the many areas of makerspace that you will be assessing in order to enrich your vision for makerspace.

ASSESSING SUPPLIES

This is an opportunity to determine whether there are enough needed supplies and whether what you have purchased is being used. The following actions offer an array of options to help you assess your supplies:

- When ordering supplies, keep the purchase orders and packing slips organized so that you can use this information for inventory and reordering purposes.
- Make a complete list of everything you ordered, and do a periodic written or visual inventory of supplies.
- Take pictures to help keep track of your observations if you are not keeping a formal log. You may notice that some supplies were in high demand and got used up while others went untouched.
- Survey students to see what their favorite supply is and to find out what new supplies they would like to see in makerspace. It can be a formal survey through a site such as Survey Monkey, or an informal venue such as a suggestion box, a large poster where they can list ideas, or sticky notes that they can add to a chart.

Taking a critical look at the results of your inventory is the next step. High-demand items that have gotten used up may be things that seem intuitive or easier to use, be placed in a prime location, or may be more colorful, popular, versatile, or connected to a curriculum area that is touched on by many grade levels. Items that seem to be left untouched may be harder to use, require more time on task, be harder to find or get to, need teacher or adult assistance, or be less appealing to students. Take this opportunity to talk with students and staff about what they notice, and compare their observations to yours.

Consider placing less-used items in a more prominent location, making a sample project using more complex materials, displaying clear instructions for how to use more difficult supplies, and have a lunch-and-learn for students and/or staff to explore more time-consuming materials to create experts who can share their knowledge with others. Replace well-used items so students can continue to use what they are comfortable with, and encourage students and teachers to use these items in new ways that enhance learning.

When creating your budget for the next year, you can use your assessment of supplies to determine what you will need to order, and what you still have on hand and don't need to reorder. Use the information you gathered to research new supplies that will enrich your makerspace, and plan to introduce these new items in a way that you believe they will be best utilized, again, based on your assessment.

ASSESSING LOCATION

Through your assessment, you may determine that a different location for makerspace is needed. You may need a larger or smaller space. The room may need to be relocated to a different place in your school building due to an increase or decrease in enrollment that causes general classrooms to be moved or reallocated. Take this into consideration when planning for the upcoming school year, and prepare a new location as needed.

You may need to review the safety features and overall layout of the new location, which provides you an opportunity to redesign and update your makerspace. Whether your space is changing locations or staying put, feature the positive aspects you uncovered while assessing supplies, and capitalize on staff and student enthusiasm to decide which items to locate prominently when reorganizing your space.

ASSESSING SCHEDULING AND ROOM USAGE

Every school's makerspace is unique; therefore, how each school utilizes makerspace in terms of scheduling, staffing, and overall room usage will vary. If you included time in makerspace as part of the master schedule for each class, you would know that each class used it when they were assigned, or close to it. If teachers were invited to sign up to use makerspace using an open calendar or sign-up sheet, keep these records to assess which classes used makerspace and during which months of the year. Going forward, you may decide to have teachers sign up to use makerspace as they believe it best fits into their class curriculum, or you may want to create a schedule for classes to use makerspace more regularly.

- Use any calendar or sign-up sheets to look for patterns, which will then inform decisions to improve makerspace. You may notice a trend where intermediate grades used makerspace more often after state or national testing was complete, or that younger graders used it around holiday time to go along with a thematic unit, for example.
- Consider tallying how often each class was there each month, or each marking period. Determine if one class was there very often and if any classes weren't in makerspace at all. This is important to do throughout the school year so that too much time doesn't go by with an unequal usage of makerspace among classes or grade levels.

Once you have some data about when classes used makerspace, use this information to help improve the program. Have informal conversations with teachers to find out why they used makerspace often or infrequently to determine what actions you can take to encourage more equal usage. You may find that a teacher who was in makerspace every week is passionate about STEAM, and it became a big part of their classroom curriculum. That teacher could then be considered a key person for other staff members to help develop your makerspace and STEAM program.

A teacher may share that they don't have enough supplies in their classroom to do projects, so they use makerspace, and therefore you would want to get more materials into their regular classroom so makerspace is used for STEAM projects and not as a supply room. A teacher may not take their class to makerspace because they are unsure of what to do or how to manage the space and materials. You can offer to help, or partner them with another teacher or staff member to encourage that teacher to dip his or her toes into the makerspace initiative.

ASSESSING STAFFING

Staffing may or may not be a concern for your makerspace. Some schools have a staff member dedicated to STEAM, others use existing staff and include STEAM and makerspace responsibilities as part of their schedule, while some schools have no staff available and rely on volunteers to run the space. Revisit your overall staffing and see if you can allocate staff to provide additional coverage for makerspace. The more often the room is available, the more students will be able to create, explore, and tinker.

Assessing staffing for makerspace depends on whether you have staff dedicated to STEAM curriculum, or what other creative uses of staff you utilized so that makerspace was made available to students. Take the following options into consideration when planning for supervision of makerspace.

- Depending on your district's requirements for supervision and what your staffing needs are, consider reallocating staff and soliciting parent volunteers to use in makerspace.
- You may be able to have a teacher on duty in makerspace along with parent volunteers before school or during recess if you plan ahead.
- If you have an extra substitute teacher available on certain days, he or she can take groups of students to makerspace as part of a project.
- Special-area teachers can do a unit of study in makerspace connected to art, music, and physical education.

Assess your available adults, as well as student helpers, to see what combinations can be made available to create student access to makerspace as often as possible.

ASSESSING PROFESSIONAL DEVELOPMENT

When you undertake a makerspace initiative, professional development is needed to introduce teachers to the philosophy, location, materials, and potential curriculum connections that are available. Each teacher approaches professional development with a different level of readiness for change and with a varying skill set for STEAM and brings a different set of experiences to the table as an educator, in general. When you assess the success of professional development related to makerspace, consider the following:

- When doing walk-throughs and formal or informal observations, notice if any maker activities are included in teachers' lessons. They may list supplies and graphic organizers that include found objects and the design process.
- Look around classrooms to see if recently completed maker activities are on display. Students may have photographs or illustrations of prototypes, or group projects related to a STEAM initiative may be in progress.
- Notice if there is a makerspace in the classroom. Appearances can range from a box of odds and ends to an organized cart of tools and supplies with ideas and instructions for projects.
- As part of a post-observation conference, discuss adding makerspace activities to upcoming lessons or as an extension to the observed lesson.

In terms of formal professional development, you will know how many workshops were officially offered and how many articles, webinars, and TED talks were suggested to staff by you and the district. What you can delve into is how many teachers sought out additional opportunities to develop makerspace activities on their own. Here are some examples to look for.

- Note which workshops teachers applied for and attended beyond what was offered to everyone.
- Some teachers may have attended Edcamps or nErDcamps on their own time, including weekends and school breaks.
- Teachers may have purchased STEAM-related books or bought subscriptions to apps or products with their own funds and are willing to share their discoveries with staff.
- Enthusiastic teachers likely have browsed Teachers Pay Teachers, Pinterest, and similar sites for makerspace activities related to the content they are teaching. You may see them making copies of what they purchased and downloaded, or setting up hands-on projects in makerspace using printouts from these resources.
- Some staff members may have applied for grants for materials and supplies from local organizations or through sites such as Donors Choose. The grant organization may contact the

teacher directly and may also send you notification of their selection of your staff member for special recognition.
- Staff may have attended, or presented at, local maker fairs and be eager to share with your faculty what they saw and/or shared. This is a way teachers may involve their own children in maker activities and can then use feedback from their family to further enhance their projects in school. If their own children were enthusiastic about an activity, there is a high likelihood that teachers will try a similar activity with their students.
- Assess teachers' involvement in professional development through conversations about what they learned and what they want to learn.

As the building administrator, you can provide opportunities for eager staff members to share their experiences and the information they gathered with colleagues. Putting together a schoolwide list of maker activities that have been done in classrooms, favorite maker-themed websites, apps, and useful workshops can inspire staff members to try new challenges, share resources, and collaborate on future projects. This is something you can do, or a teacher-leader or intern may want to take on this project.

ASSESSING STUDENT LEARNING

Intuitively we want to believe that makerspace is good for students and that students are learning by making things. However, it is essential to be able to substantiate that feeling with data. Student learning can be assessed both formally and informally in makerspace, similar to the ways assessment takes place in classrooms for reading, math, social studies, and science. Traditional worksheets and written assignments can provide insight into student learning, as can performance tasks. It is important to plan in advance so that you have opportunities to assess learning, such as having teachers include a written component to their projects, observing lessons in makerspace, and gathering artifacts such as exit tickets and photographs.

Paper-and-pencil assessment can be an integral part of assessing learning in makerspace. At the same time, it can and should be a natural outgrowth of a creative project rather than assessment for the sake of assessment. Teachers can have students fill out graphic organizers that detail the engineering process they used to create their project. This will include steps such as asking questions, listing the research information needed, sketching as part of planning and creating a design, and revising their work by explaining what they want to change and why. These worksheets will show understanding and depth of knowledge for a particular project.

Additionally, students may have sketches with notes that can be used to assess learning when there are changes to the sketches that explain the development of that student's engineering process. Students can describe, in writing, what they made and what they learned and can keep this information in an inventor's log. They can create a how-to guide for the steps needed to make their project so that other students can make the same project. This how-to guide can become part of a student project library in makerspace. These assessment pieces are all natural components of makerspace projects that are part of the process or are intended to be for an authentic audience, which can also be used to measure student learning.

Students can be assessed through video or audio recordings about their learning, as long as parent permission is obtained. You can work with teachers to create individual video clips or a montage of many students showing their projects and explaining what they learned. Share videos with an authentic audience of parents and other students, as well as posting it to your school's website to demonstrate learning that is taking place in makerspace. You can also turn a video into a QR (quick response) code and send the QR image home as part of a school newsletter so families can view the video on handheld devices as well as sharing their child's makerspace learning with others who may be farther away.

On a smaller scale, exit tickets can be used to assess learning in makerspace. At the end of a project, students can be offered an exit ticket where they can write down what they learned that day and what they would like to learn in makerspace in the future. You can connect the exit ticket to your larger philosophy of learning and enrichment by asking students to write down how they can use their makerspace experience to make the world a better place.

They can use this higher-order thinking opportunity to extend their learning beyond the school walls. Students may say they are now confident to try new things, will use this skill to become entrepreneurs and make and sell items for profit, have thought of a new career they are interested in, or will create projects to donate to those in need. Gather the exit slips for a particular project and note all students' responses to the questions in a list or chart, and you will notice words, terms, and ideas that are frequently used. This information is thematic data, and can be used to assess the project, materials, and process involved in makerspace assignments.

For makerspace projects, you may consider using a rubric for students to use for self-assessment and to guide them through the engineering process. You can create a rubric as a school to use in makerspace generically, or a teacher may want to create a project-specific rubric. Include the steps in the design and engineering process and keep it simple, at least to begin with. The goal is for students to be successful and learn in which areas they can still personally develop further. A rubric may also be useful for a group project, or one with many steps that takes a longer period of time, to help keep track of the project and its participants.

ASSESSING COMMUNITY INVOLVEMENT

Parents, local businesses, and PTA organizations may play a role in supplying, organizing, and helping supervise your makerspace. As the year progresses, it is important for you to assess their participation in order to make adjustments or plans for the months ahead. Determine how involved the parents are by noting if they participate in any of the following activities.

- send in supply donations when requests are sent out
- join a makerspace committee or send in ideas to use
- spend time in makerspace organizing items
- volunteer their time to assist from home by preparing materials or projects
- make contacts in the community who can help expand makerspace opportunities

Each community has differing resources depending on tangible and intangible factors. If parents and family members have any amount of time, a related skill set, or useful supplies that can be donated to makerspace, it will benefit the students if you encourage participation in a variety of ways. Often working parents, parents who are ill or who are caretakers, those with fewer resources, or those with younger children might feel disconnected from school-participation opportunities. Makerspace lends itself to including everyone who is interested since help can be in such a wide range of forms.

ASSESSING YOUR PROFESSIONAL GROWTH

Taking on makerspace as the building principal is a significant project, with potentially rewarding experiences for you, your staff, and students. As you assess the various aspects of makerspace, it is important to assess your own growth to ensure that you don't stagnate and continue doing the same thing over again. Think about the professional development opportunities you may have experienced throughout the creation and implementation of makerspace, and consider ways to apply your learning to your larger role as the lead learner.

- Did you discover new materials, supplies, and vendors? You can now use that information across the curriculum to help teachers find additional resources. Companies will send you catalogs and discounts, especially at the beginning of the school year. Review these resources by checking for online reviews, contacting colleagues, or ordering a small amount of an item to see if what companies are offering will be appropriate for your school.
- Have you become more comfortable with technology, apps, and robots and/or coding than you were before you began the makerspace initiative? You can confidently share your learning firsthand with staff members who may have been timid about technology through faculty meetings, lunch-and-learn sessions, or informal lessons or demonstrations where teachers can explore this technology with your support. Join groups of like-minded educators who share new knowledge about cutting-edge innovations, read professionally, and contribute to the existing body of knowledge about technology in elementary education.
- Did you attend workshops; read professional books, blogs, and articles; watch TED talks; follow Twitter feeds; and/or seek out maker events? Immersing yourself in maker culture will expose you to many ideas, products, and materials so that you can confidently select what is just right for your school community.
- Become a resource to your school community by staying current regarding makerspace ideas and materials. Share what you learn via staff newsletters, e-mail blasts, and tweets so that your teachers can use your learning as a springboard for their own growth. Encourage teachers to attend workshops

and suggest relevant articles and books or excerpts that will help staff embrace STEAM in a way that works best for them.
- Create a space such as a tangible or electronic bulletin board for staff to share their resources, including favorite apps, articles, and websites that inspire their projects and plans, and be sure to include your findings there as well.
- Just as we encourage students to share their learning with an authentic audience, find opportunities to share your learning with colleagues. Provide a workshop for staff in your district for sharing your experiences. Consider submitting a proposal to be a presenter at a local conference or join a conversation on social media such as Twitter or a blog about makerspace or STEAM.

Teachers, students, and parents will look to you to be an enthusiastic supporter of makerspace. Developing yourself as a learner and leader is vital because you will serve as a role model of lifelong learning for your constituents. Your professional growth can pave the way for the future of your school's makerspace, and possibly for the scope of real-world applications that your students will be prepared to take advantage of as they grow up and reflect on their early years as makers, tinkerers, and creators.

EIGHT

The Journey Ahead

As you venture into makerspace, both literally and figuratively, you will be creating transdisciplinary opportunities for students to become involved in the design and engineering process. Rather than a unit being interdisciplinary where, for example, when learning about bears, students will create an art project, experience a book about hibernation, and separately map where different types of bears live, units that include makerspace will encourage students to work on projects that inherently weave together science, technology, engineering, art, and math concepts without distinguishing among the content areas. You will continue to be the driving force behind the growth of your makerspace with each improvement you make, and at the same time shape the collaborative, creative, and process-oriented climate of your school.

The expression, "A rising tide raises all ships," applies to the growth of makerspace. Having high expectations for yourself and the ways in which you develop your program can result in an increased quality of experiences for all students. Model ways to use makerspace with learners of all ages and abilities, and demonstrate that this is a place where success for all is possible.

As the journey to improve makerspace continues, the balance of teaching and learning shifts among staff and students. Makerspace projects humble us as we reflect on the concept that students and staff are all teachers, and we are all learners, just at different points in the process.

As principal, keeping the lines of communication open is important so that teachers feel comfortable sharing their successes and challenges with each other and with you and that you do the same. If something goes well, celebrate! If a product, project, or plan doesn't work out, share that, too. Use these opportunities to demonstrate how to evaluate and improve upon a program, and to model self-reflection and goal setting.

After you bring makerspace to your school, and assess and adjust as necessary, what can you do next? The journey ahead can go in different directions, depending on your available resources. Every school year brings new demands, both locally and nationally, that need to be met. Each year brings new challenges regarding student and staff needs. Each start of the school year brings the chance for a new beginning, for a fresh outlook, and the opportunity to grow existing initiatives into bigger and better programs.

Makerspace can serve as a vehicle for moving your school forward, absorbing demands and challenges, and turning difficulties into triumphs. To move this initiative forward, it is important to reach beyond the borders of the actual makerspace. Some ways you can advance your program are suggested here:

- Compare the new science standards that are being adopted or adapted by your state to your school's current science curriculum. Find ways that your makerspace can meet the new science and engineering requirements and develop lessons and units of study that bridge the gap, connecting makerspace philosophy with the new crosscutting expectations.
- To grow the reach of your makerspace, videoconference with scientists or with makers at another school. Share projects and ideas across time zones, borders, and languages.
- Challenge teachers and students in creative contests such as the most innovative way to use a clothespin or to make a new product using just four items. You might get some innovative ideas for challenges that can be readily adapted to makerspace projects from Odyssey of the Mind materials that are publicly available.
- Work with teachers to develop lessons that encourage divergent thinking, brainstorming, and a flexible mindset in their content area units of study. Model these types of experiences with staff to encourage the positive outcomes that can be seen in students, such as increased confidence, teamwork, im-

proved listening skills, more relevant responses, and having multiple solutions to a problem.
- Ask community members to share how their careers connect to the design process, and have those people present workshops to students as an assembly before or after school or during lunchtime. Students might want to follow up with questions and show their appreciation with a thank-you note sharing what they learned or how they were inspired.
- Connect with local universities to see what programs might be available to your school, often at little to no cost. For example, Stony Brook University has student organizations that are eager to bring engineering programs to local schools.
- A local BOCES (Boards of Cooperative Education Services) has a STEAM van that comes to member schools, bringing robotics, coding, and other hands-on electronic activities to students, along with knowledgeable staff to facilitate learning. A museum in Staten Island has a Makerspace Mobile. If there isn't one near you, you can create one or work with your local library to create one, like the bookmobiles of days past.
- Take students on field trips to expand your makerspace offerings. Investigate programs at a local library, museum, art gallery, nature preserve, and even a roller rink or movie theater. Many have devised programs that are centered on STEAM activities, and you can use a makerspace experience as a preview or follow-up to the trip.
- If going out on a field trip is not an option, bring field trips in. Companies, such as Mad Science and others, can set up in a large space or do classroom workshops for your students.
- Invest in STEAM curriculum after careful investigation and with district approval. When you first begin makerspace, take some time to evaluate your school's resources and needs before diving in and making a decision and/or purchasing content. See what you need to align to current curriculum standards.

Many companies offer grade-level-specific units of study that include reproducibles with step-by-step instructions and supply lists for projects related to topics such as weather, animals, nutrition, space, and forces. Other companies have boxed programs that contain all of the materials needed for a class set of projects such as solar vehicles, egg drop launchers, rockets, and catapults.

You need to decide if you are going to purchase consumable or non-consumable items, and spending some time with a makerspace that begins as an Exploratorium, for students and teachers, will guide you to make the best decision. Consider the readiness level of your staff; find a program such as Project Lead the Way, Science 21, or Smithsonian, which seem teacher friendly.

- Have a STEAM night where parents and their children sign up to participate in an extended project, such as learning how to code, use stop-motion animation, or experiment with magnets. Teachers or parent volunteers can facilitate each project, and families can rotate systematically through the activities.
- Host a maker fair at your school. Invite parents and students to the school after hours to visit a variety of booths that have simple maker activities at each. Use makerspace projects that have been successful throughout the school year, and use supplies that you have a large stock of. Create instructions and sample projects, and have volunteers assist at each booth. Involve the middle school and high school if they have honor societies or community service clubs where students earn credit for helping at events. Request parent volunteers, and hold an informational meeting ahead of time. Create a map of which activities are where, and send students home with a small bag of supplies so they can continue to be makers. Consider a theme for the fair, or use your school mascot to unite the event.
- Stay organized. Keep a log or journal of your adventures as you create makerspace in your school. Take photographs of students creating their inventions. Keep sample copies of students' sketches and plans. Put professional articles that you share with staff into a binder for future reference. Maintain a professional library of books for staff about creativity, making and tinkering, enrichment, STEAM, and project ideas.

When considering which actions you will choose to follow in order to bring makerspace to your school and then to utilize to continue to grow and enhance your program, remain true to your educational philosophy, and focus on why you became a school administrator. Let those passions guide your initiative. Serving as a resource, putting children first, valuing community involvement, and leading a school through changes in curriculum standards to effect positive changes are all possible through makerspace.

Appendix

RESOURCES

This section offers suggested lists, letters, and ideas for you to use with students, staff, and families as you develop your makerspace. You might want to add graphics, interesting fonts, and borders to catch your readers' attention as you refer to these documents and adjust them to fit your school's needs. The following resources can be found here:

- Sample Notice to Parents and Staff Introducing Makerspace
- Sample Supply List to Send Home with Students
- Sample Sign-Up Sheet for Makerspace Recess Projects
- Sample of Data from Exit Tickets
- Makerspace Mind Map Graphic Organizer
- Picture Book List to Inspire Creative Thinking
- Rubric for Makerspace Projects
- Sample Exit Ticket
- Vendors for STEAM Supplies

Continue to research and create your own resource library with new books and articles that become available. Share resources with your staff, and work together to tailor information so that it benefits your students and enriches your Makerspace.

SAMPLE NOTICE TO PARENTS AND STAFF INTRODUCING MAKERSPACE

Coming Soon to Our Elementary School: Makerspace
What is Makerspace?

Makerspace can be a unique area in our school that allows for creativity and innovation to occur. Students have the freedom to design, engineer, fabricate, create, build, and collaborate to make tangible objects that connect to learning standards while proving to be hands-on opportunities to explore new tools, processes, and ideas. We are starting rather low tech and thinking big! The Maker Movement incorporates STEAM initiatives: science, technology, engineering, art, and mathematics.

Why do we need Makerspace?

Working in the Makerspace engages students to think critically and problem solve in ways that deepen their knowledge of subject matter. Makerspace opportunities improve students' habits of inquiry, self-directed learning, and reflection. Students will have a way of learning that involves tinkering, inventing, researching, teaching, collaborating, sharing, innovating, socializing, and creating. Students develop new ideas, design and redesign them until they have a product they are happy with that in some way solves a problem, shares new information, and connects to the content area, and ultimately they learn things about themselves and the world. Makers are needed to add to the global sum of human knowledge — we can start now!

When and how will Makerspace be used?

This is a work in progress. Makerspaces are in the works for the library, possibly the computer lab, and also a newly available small space. All classes and all students will have opportunities to be Makers. Materials/resources may also be available for use in classroom projects. We hope to begin with an Exploratorium, where all students will get to tinker with the items available and take it from there.

Who is involved in Makerspace?

Students, staff, and parents are all partners in creating and utilizing a successful Makerspace. We will have a Makerspace committee made up of staff, students, and parents to help develop this dynamic idea. We will add supplies and resources over time and evaluate its success as we go.

How can you be part of Makerspace and the *Maker Movement* in general?

If you have a few seconds: gather items and donate them as supplies to be used in our Makerspace. We will be collecting items from students/families beginning soon.

If you have a few minutes: check out some websites that have ideas for things to make—feel free to share ideas for our Makerspace Resource Library or make them with your class. Some great sites include Instructables.com, Designmaketeach.com, DIY.org, and Makered.org.

If you have a few hours: become a teacher member of the Makerspace Committee and help us gather resources and supplies to grow our space! You can also create a mini-makerspace in your classroom as an enrichment-for-all opportunity!

SAMPLE SUPPLY LIST TO SEND HOME WITH STUDENTS

Makerspace Donations Needed

Building Toys	Craft Supplies	Electrical Items
Tinkertoys	Crayons	Watch batteries
K'Nex	Markers	LED lights
Lego (especially people and wheels)	Buttons	Thin wire
	Lanyard	Copper tape
Bristle Blocks	Rainbow loom supplies	Adhesives
Connectors	Looms/hot loops	Painter's tape
Binder clips	Felt	Electrical tape
Clothespins	Yarn	Glue
Rubber bands	Thread	Packing tape
Brads	Embroidery floss	Duck or duct tape
Bobby pins	Empty film canisters	Masking tape
Safety pins	Empty spools (from thread or ribbon)	Household Items
Paper		Styrofoam cups
Origami paper	Pipe cleaners	Small bathroom cups
Tracing paper	Popsicle sticks	Empty toilet paper rolls
Tissue paper	Cross-stitch material	Ziplock bags
Construction paper	Sewing needles	Brown paper lunch bags
Tools	Crochet hooks	Straws
Wire cutters	Knitting needles	Plastic bottle caps
Scissors	Ribbon	Toothpicks
Hole punchers	Small kids craft sewing machine	Trading cards
Rulers		Velcro
Pliers	Batting/stuffing	Plastic spoons
Measuring tape	Fuse beads and pattern boards	Paint stirrers
		Other
	Googly eyes	Tiny rubber balls
	Stickers	Marbles
	Beads	
	Wire or elastic for beads	

SAMPLE SIGN-UP SHEET FOR MAKERSPACE RECESS PROJECTS

Name _____ Teacher_____

Makerspace Sign-Up

In February, we will be having workshops for special projects. There will also be days that Makerspace will be open for your own creative ideas. These will all take place during your recess and lunchtime.

Please <u>put a checkmark next to 2 projects you REALLY want to do</u>, and we will send your teachers a schedule so you'll know what day(s) to come.

Workshops

____ **Emoji Explorations**: You will design, cut, sew, and stuff a unique emoji pillow. This workshop is great for anyone who is interested in fashion design, cartooning, and being a doctor or veterinarian who may need to know how to stitch.

____ **Trading Card Creations**: You will use trading cards (like baseball and football cards, Pokemon cards, Minion cards, and others) to make useful items like wallets, bookmarks, and notepads. This workshop is great for anyone who likes to collect, recycle, and make gifts for themselves and others.

____ **Open Makerspace**: Use your imagination to plan, design, make, and improve your own new project using materials we have. This workshop is great for inventors, engineers, designers, planners, and crafters.

____ **Pixel Mania**: Use fuse beads to make pixelated designs such as animals, vehicles, video game characters, and more. This workshop is great for artists, gamers, animators, and crafters.

____ **Yarn Fun**: Make dolls, snowballs, cupcakes, and scarves. This workshop is great for anyone who likes to work with their hands and follow a pattern.

SAMPLE OF DATA COLLECTED LISTING 4TH AND 5TH GRADERS' RESPONSES ON EXIT TICKETS FROM AN EMOJI PILLOW MAKERSPACE PROJECT

Write a word that describes how you felt in Makerspace today.
Awesome
Excited
Confused
Happy
Amazing
Creative

What did you learn today?
How to sew
How to make a pillow
How to make something in a short time
I can spend time away from TV
Anything is possible if you sew
To make things with scraps
How to knot thread
That you can make simple stuff to make something cool

How can you use what you learned to make the world a better place?
I can sew cuts if I'm a doctor
To donate to charity
To give them to people in hospitals to make them feel happy
I can sew ripped things
I can make pillows and blankets for the homeless
I can make clothes to keep people warm
I can make a business of this
I can make useful things
I can use scraps to make something
I can teach other people how to sew

MAKERSPACE MIND MAP GRAPHIC ORGANIZER

Makerspace Mind Map

- Ask
- Imagine
- Plan
- Create
- Improve

PICTURE BOOK LIST TO INSPIRE CREATIVE THINKING

Barnett, Mac. (2012). *Extra Yarn*. Balzer and Bray.
Beatty, Andrea. (2016). *Ada Twist, Scientist*. Abrams Books for Young Readers.
Beatty, Andrea. (2010). *Iggy Peck, Architect*. Abrams Books for Young Readers.
Beatty, Andrea. (2013). *Rosie Revere, Engineer*. Abrams Books for Young Readers.
Breen, Steve. (2008). *Violet the Pilot*. Penguin Young Readers Group.
Matthews, Elizabeth. (2007). *Different Like Coco*. Candlewick Press.
McCully, Emily. (2006). *Marvelous Mattie*. Farrar, Straus and Giroux.
Polacco, Patricia. (2010). *The Junkyard Wonders*. Philomel Books.
Reynolds, Peter, and Paul Reynolds. (2014). *Going Places*. Atheneum Books for Young Readers.
Reynolds, Peter. (2004). *Ish*. Candlewick Press.
Reynolds, Peter. (2003). *The Dot*. Candlewick Press.
Riddell, Chris. (2010). *Wendell's Workshop*. Katherine Tegen Books.
Santat, Dan. (2014). *The Adventures of Beekle*. Little, Brown Books for Young Readers.
Spires, Ashley. (2014). *The Most Magnificent Thing*. Kids Can Press, Limited.
Vida, Frank. (2013). *Young Frank*. The Museum of Modern Art.
Yamada, Kobi. (2014). *What Do You Do with an Idea?* Compendium.

SAMPLE EXIT TICKET FOR A MAKERSPACE PROJECT

Exit Ticket

Name _____ Date _____

Makerspace Project _____

What step(s) in the design and engineering process did you find most helpful and why?

_____

_____

What skills or strategies did you learn while making this project?

_____

_____

What would you like to make next?

_____

_____

How can you use what you learned to make the world a better place?

_____

_____

VENDORS FOR STEAM SUPPLIES

Here is an alphabetical list of vendors that sell STEAM supplies. This is not an endorsement of any company but is intended to be a resource to help administrators begin to research and purchase supplies for makerspace. You might want to begin by browsing their sites or paging through their catalogs to get an overview of the range and price of their available products. Some are national retail chains, some offer school discounts, and others are sole-source vendors.

Amazon
Barnes and Noble
Bloxels
Carolina
Delta
Discovery
K'Nex
Lakeshore Learning
Lego
Littlebits
Makershed
Makeymakey
Michael's
Nasco
Oriental Trading
Ozobot
Pitsco
Scholastic
School Specialty
Sparkfun
Stemfinity
Target
Tiggly
Thinkgeek
Uline
Walmart

References

Bevan, Bronwyn, Mike Petrich, and Karen Wilkinson. 2014/2015. "Tinkering Is Serious Play." *Educational Leadership*. December/January: 28–33.
Boss, Suzie. 2011. "Project-Based Learning: A Short History." September 20. http://www.edutopia.org/project-based-learning-history.
Brooks, Jacqueline G., and Martin G. Brooks. 1993. *In Search of Understanding: The Case for Constructivist Classrooms*. Alexandria, VA: Association for Supervision and Curriculum Development.
Drapeau, Patti. 2014. *Sparking Student Creativity: Practical Ways to Promote Innovative Thinking and Problem Solving*. Alexandria, VA: Association for Supervision and Curriculum Development.
Dweck, Carol. 2007. *Mindset: The New Psychology of Success*. New York: Random House.
Fleming, Laura. 2015. *Worlds of Making: Best Practices for Establishing a Makerspace for Your School*. Thousand Oaks, CA: Corwin.
Gruenert, Steve. 2008. "School Culture, School Climate: They Are Not the Same Thing." *Principal*. March/April: 56–59.
Hlubinka, Michelle, Dale Dougherty, Parker Thomas, Stephanie Chang, Steve Hoefer, Isaac Alexander, and Devon McGuire. 2013. *Makerspace Playbook*. Maker Media. www.makerspace.com.
Loukas, Alexandra. 2007. "What Is School Climate?" *Leadership Compass*. 5(1):1–3.
Mraz, Kristine, and Christine Hertz. 2015. *A Mindset for Learning: Teaching the Traits of Joyful, Independent Growth*. Portsmouth, NH: Heinemann.
Piaget, Jean. 1973. *To Understand Is to Invent: The Future of Education*. New York: Grossman Publishers.
Renzulli, Joseph. 1998. "Enrichment Learning and Teaching." *Tools for Schools*. April. http://www2.ed.gov/pubs/ToolsforSchools/sem.html.

About the Author

Randee Bonagura, EdD, is an elementary school principal in New York. She has been active in the field of education for twenty years. Bonagura received her bachelor of arts degree from Hofstra University and began her career as an elementary school teacher on Long Island. After earning her master of science in school administration, she served as a Reading Department supervisor and taught literacy and math to middle and high school students as well as provided professional development to staff. Bonagura completed her doctorate in literacy studies and was an adjunct professor at Hofstra University and Dowling College, then went on to become an assistant principal.

www.ingramcontent.com/pod-product-compliance
Lightning Source LLC
Chambersburg PA
CBHW021801230426
43669CB00006B/156